THE REHEARSAL HANDBOOK
FOR ACTORS AND DIRECTORS

A PRACTICAL GUIDE

The REHEARSAL HANDBOOK

for actors and directors

John Perry

The Crowood Press

First published in 2001 by
The Crowood Press Ltd
Ramsbury, Marlborough
Wiltshire SN8 2HR

British Library Cataloguing-in-Publication Data
A catalogue record for this book is available from the British Library.

ISBN 1 86126 443 7

Acknowledgements
I would like to thank the directors Andrew Visnevski, Andrew Norton, Deborah
Yhip, Philip Hoffman, Catherine Clouzot, Nic Tudor and Robert Horwell, and their
companies of actors, for their generosity in allowing me to photograph their
rehearsals, and also Di Stedman and her team. The support of the School of Acting
at the ArtsEd, London, is very much appreciated. I would like to thank Judy Farrar
for encouraging me to write this.

Photographs by Panos Velliantatis, Ian Stern and the author.

Line drawings by Annette Findlay.

Front cover: Lorraine Stanley and Louise Appel rehearsing *Say What?*, dir. Andrew
Norton. Photo: Panos Velliantatis.
Back cover: Edward E. Eiriksson rehearsing *Man of La Mancha*, dir. Nic Tudor. Photo:
John Perry.

Typefaces used: Cheltenham Bold Condensed (chapter headings), Photina MT (main
text) and Helvetica (labels).

Typeset and designed by D & N Publishing
Baydon, Marlborough, Wiltshire.

Printed and bound in Great Britain by JW Arrowsmith, Bristol.

CONTENTS

PREFACE

This is a little book about a huge subject. It is a sourcebook for actors, directors and theatre makers who are in the process of developing their individual working practices. The book is a toolbox of approaches and exercises.

There are now Masters degrees in directing, acting and every other aspect of theatre, but many jobbing directors still don't go to school to learn their craft. They begin by taking on directing jobs, often heartened by personal experiences of dreadful directing, and then they pick up skills as they go along, learning by watching others, since many directors begin as actors or stage managers. Once they are established, however, it's rare for them to watch each other work, so there are almost as many different directing styles as there are directors. A director may or may not understand the technicalities of stagecraft; he or she may or may not be able to facilitate actors; they may turn out to be an incompetent visionary or an uninspiring but competent manager; they may inspire actors by frightening them, or by behaving with such pathetic childishness that the actor feels obliged to help them through the rehearsal process. This book is an attempt to create signposts for directors who are starting out, by suggesting first steps, plans of action and the way to make creative progress with actors.

The last section of this book suggests some independent work that actors can do alone or with colleagues, as part of the rehearsal process. However good or bad the director, it is important that actors, while working within the director's vision, retain a strong sense of artistic independence. Without this it is difficult for the actor to work with that feeling of ownership and responsibility that is at the root of a committed performance.

Experienced practitioners might find this book useful as an easy-reference set of notes. Rehearsal is a secret art, so planning it can be a lonely business. This is true of formal rehearsals and of the actor's private preparation. To walk into the rehearsal room often feels like an intrusion on an intimate personal encounter, so many novice directors and actors have no idea how those outside their own circles work, and the range of options aren't always evident when projects are planned. This book is designed to be one half of a dialogue in the mind of the reader, suggesting procedures, encouraging exploration and provoking a response. This sort of dialogue is necessary and helpful when you have to plan workshops and rehearsals alone. I hope the book will help directors and actors deal with this, the least communal aspect of a highly communal art.

First principles and process are emphasized, and the reader will test these through practice. Nobody ever became an actor or a director by reading a book, doing a degree or taking training. Practice is everything, and there is no easy recipe for putting on plays, or for solving the problems they present. In fact it is necessary to find new methods for each new project – to invent and reinvent. This is the best part of the work.

This book is entirely about preparation – sometimes even about preparing for preparation.

Rehearsal moments (dir. Andrew Norton).

There's hardly a word about performance in it, except as context. The audience – the whole object of rehearsal – is hardly mentioned. In fact, this book is about first steps, rather than delivery. I assume that readers are familiar with performance, and if not can easily go and see some. There are already plenty of good books on acting, some of which feature in the Bibliography. Rehearsal, being private, is more difficult to access and there are not many books on it other than studies of the great practitioners. It is also very difficult to describe, since the most mechanical moments in a rehearsal are rarely the most significant. Often very slight exchanges, only significant in retrospect, deeply affect an actor's sense of character, motivation or the world of the play. This process is of interest in its own right, but it must serve the interests of performance and the audience, otherwise it is merely bad therapy.

A word about the audience. Consider a collection of observers who might visit, for example, an art gallery. These individuals would turn into an audience if suddenly confronted by a shocking exhibit, which caused an involuntary collective response. They would respond both as individuals and, perhaps differently, as an audience. An audience has a collective character; it is an animal in its own right, quite distinct from the individual characters that make it up. Furthermore, the audience is *active*. It makes a positive contribution to the action. Its presence is felt strongly on the stage. It actually affects the performance, which will change under the collective gaze. No two performances are the same because no two audiences respond in the same way. This is true both of a bunch of cabaret hecklers and a middle-class audience sitting politely in the dark. The audience doesn't have to do anything in order to palpably affect a performance. The focus of its collective attention – or lack of it – is sufficient. When theatre is at its best, the performers and the audience are engaging in a succession of intense emotional incidents, the actors playing totally to each other, as if they are alone, yet aware that they are observed. This is one of many simultaneous double truths that are the essence of the live theatre experience. When the performance is over, it leaves absolutely no evidence behind it, except traces in the memories of the actors and audience. Performance then, is like cookery: long and detailed preparation, followed by the intense and all too brief experience of consumption, followed by endless discussions, trying to recollect whether or not it was any good.

The implications for rehearsal are significant. The audience cannot possibly be replicated in the rehearsal room. The director attempts to behave like a responsive and articulate audience but can never truly do this, because he or she is too familiar with the production to respond spontaneously and, being only one person, cannot imitate a collective force.

Rehearsals are therefore conducted under the shadow of this partner, which is made more powerful by its absence. A date will have been set upon which the audience will join in and make the creative moment complete. That date by tradition is carved in stone – the show must go on. As this date approaches and rehearsal time dwindles away, it becomes the director's job to 'hold the space', that is, to behave towards the company as though there were plenty of rehearsal time available. This must be done if the rehearsal is not to collapse into hysterical chaos. The director slowly lets go of the production, putting it into the hands of the actors and technicians. When opening night arrives, the redundancy of the director is complete, and it is the presence of the audience that turns the private, domestic, secret society of the rehearsal room into a public event.

John Perry is Head of Development and Partnership at the ArtsEd, London. He can be contacted at johnperry@prometheus.fsnet.co.uk.

PART ONE

REHEARSALS, ANCIENT AND MODERN

Performance is the great social art. It rejects the insularity and privacy of the poet or the painter and seeks self-expression though relationship. Each performance is a three-layered collaborative network of artists, consisting first of specialist writers, designers, choreographers and directors; second of a community of performing artists; and last but not least of the audience, who become imaginative artists for the purpose of experiencing the performance.

Consider possible roles that feature in each collaboration. Should the actor be passive, like putty moulded by the director, or active and opinionated? Will the new century create a new artist to replace the director, as the director has replaced the actor-manager? The potential for developing the roles of collaborating artists and their relationship offers infinite creative possibility.

These relationships are a great creative variable in the art of theatre, and the purpose of the first part of this book is to give the reader a sense of its range. This is done by looking at history and at the contemporary scene, and by examining assumptions concerning the actor–director relationship. There follows a description of the conventional production process.

Having thus created a context for the chapters that follow, this part of the book will encourage the reader to question all assumptions regarding the roles and relationships necessary for theatre. Beyond the simple action of the performer on the spectator, nothing need be taken for granted.

1 REHEARSAL – HISTORICAL ANECDOTES

NOTHING STAYS THE SAME

The elements of theatre – writing, staging, acting style, audience relationship, lighting, sound, director's concept, relationship to the audience and the social and political setting – combine in a rich and powerful language. Like all living languages, theatre is in a state of constant evolution and its conventions are only obvious in hindsight or at a distance. For example, Sarah Bernhardt's nineteenth-century 'operatic' acting style seemed glorious to her contemporaries but drew howls of derision from twentieth-century actors trained in the 'method', who prefer what they would call a more 'truthful' approach. However, this 'truth', based in realism, now appears to be passing as theatre clowns and puppets re-emerge from the wings of the contemporary stage. Modern acting theory, seeking once more to redefine itself, looks backward to the future.

Because, after the performance, the play survives only as folk memory or play text, it is easy to believe that the play, even the playwright, is a vital element of the theatre. In fact, literature accounts for only a tiny fraction of the history of stage productions. The improvised theatre produced by pre-literate cultures is lost to history, as is every subsequent unrecorded impro, mime, spectacle or busker's turn.

Contemporary theatre seems to be the property of the director, yet the director's role is a very recent addition to the production team, a convention that may prove to be passing. Many young theatre makers now see play texts and the conventional organization of the production process not as absolutes, but as choices in a range of possibilities, even as old-fashioned habits.

Theatre is a live and constantly evolving collaborative art, and all collaborations beyond the basic relationship between actors and their audience are choices. The most creative approach to a production is empirical, actors and directors behaving towards each production as though it was absolutely unique, assuming that there are no rules but bringing their experience of previous work to bear on each issue as it arises.

Theatre is a social art and is moulded by the culture that surrounds it. All societies require leisure time and wealth beyond subsistence-level if they are to produce art at all, especially theatre, which combines many arts. Rehearsal is an even greater luxury than performance, requiring even greater surplus of time, money and interest, and an audience or benefactor capable of paying back the investment. The exploratory, team-building, devising, trial-and-error nature of rehearsal is very modern, and can be distinguished from 'practice', which consists of blocking (*see* page 46) and line learning, and is relatively cheap and quick.

What follows are some historical snapshots of Western practice, intended to demonstrate some of the practical issues that shape the conventions of theatre practice.

The theatre maker's blank page.

REHEARSAL IN WESTERN THEATRE: A NOTEBOOK

Sacred Drama – the Writer/Actor as Director, Priest and Chorus Leader

Traditional societies use art – all of the arts – as part of the highly practical process of survival. The Neolithic paintings at Lascaux, whose deer and charging bulls come to life on the cave walls in the flickering light of lamp oil, seem to be created not as a leisure activity but as an attempt to forge an alliance with God. Humans forge and renew relationships with natural gods and spirits of the forces of nature over which they have no control.

Performance in this setting is combined art. Body decoration with paints and with objects combine with movement and dance, elicited by rhythm and music. At its most sophisticated level, the leader transforms – or is transformed – into the hunter or the hunted animal by means of costume and characterful signs and movement.

Traditional theatre of this kind takes place in a world where the actual landscape and the landscape of the imagination are indistinguishable. Performance is therefore not separated from real life, but is its ultimate expression. The actor is an actor-priest – a protagonist who acts out imaginatively an important tribal venture, or is a midwife to tribal dreams and desires. The essence of acting in this type of theatre is to become possessed by the character. An actor-priest does not construct a character like a modern actor, but instead becomes totally empty in order to receive the spirit of the god or demi-god who is being brought onto the stage.

12

Rehearsal Features of 'Sacred' Drama

- It is religious and contains the ritual elements of offering and sacrifice.
- Performance combines the arts of painting, poetry, dance, music, song, landscape, architecture and acting.
- Preparation is prescribed, traditional, ritualized and sacred.
- Movement and dance are organized as a formalized language of gesture, which must be learned.
- The drama often features a chorus. This sometimes consists of performers, sometimes of onlookers. The main actor has dialogue with the chorus.
- The tradition is oral rather than literary. Therefore the language is poetic and rhythmic, as an aid to accurate memorization.
- Ritual preparation is invariably secret. The onlookers (audience) are not allowed to see the secret parts of the drama.
- Preparation is focused on preparing the actor-priest to be possessed by the character portrayed in the ritual.

Traditional ritual theatre was successfully commercialized in the fifth century BC by the Greeks, whose themes derived from the *Odyssey* and the *Iliad* of Homer. Aeschylus and Sophocles, the writers and main actors, were also priests of Dionysus, chorus leaders and trainers of the chorus. In this context, rehearsal is the accurate and sincere re-creation of traditional form. There is a language of gesture, movement and dance, and rules and conventions of tradition bind the drama. The killing of the tragic lead harks back to religious sacrifice.

Performance without Rehearsal – 'Entrances and Exits'

Elizabethan actors did rehearse, but probably not in the sense that we would understand it. Playwrights sold manuscripts to companies who then owned them outright. The actors' speeches would then be transcribed from the manuscript so that they had only their own speeches plus cue lines. This was done because it was cheaper than copying out full scripts by hand, and also so that actors would not be tempted to sell their copy of the script to a rival company as their own work, since copyright hadn't yet been invented. The actor's script was called a 'part script' or 'cue script', and the practice of rehearsing using these 'sides' as they came to be called, persisted into the last century. There was also a 'Platt' or 'action plot', created from the manuscript. This was a list of the scenes, the characters in it, the action, sometimes including notes regarding props and costume. It was hung up backstage so that the actors knew when, where and how to come on and what they should carry onto the stage.

We know very little about Elizabethan acting style, so this speculation makes use of anecdote and the scant evidence:

- 'Acting' consisted of 'declamation' (clear and impassioned speech) and 'mime' (a system of signs indicating emotional states).
- Conventions governing movement and positioning on stage served as do-it-yourself blocking.
- The actors may or may not have rendered the script faithfully. Comics apparently did not, shamelessly busking the text, milking an appreciative crowd and getting off quick if they weren't getting laughs.

13

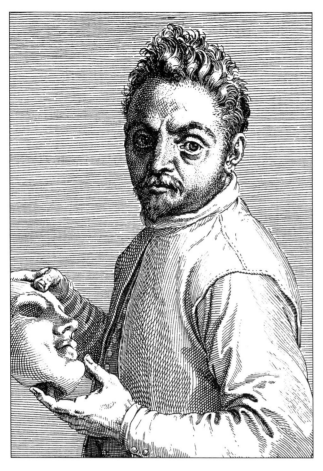

The actor Jean Gabrielle with his mask.

- Taking place in an open-air street-theatre atmosphere, it is likely that bold story-telling was more important than consistent style.
- Presumably boy apprentices, who played the women, picked up pragmatic solutions to acting problems from their masters.
- A conventional language of gesture and movement would certainly have helped young boys to play complex female roles such as Cleopatra, much as a virtuoso child might play a symphony.

- If, as seems likely, all the actors understood the conventions of how to move around the stage, rehearsal time could be cut right back, being a mere run through of entrances and exits.
- It would have been essential to stage a play in minimal time since new plays were in great demand and produced at an extraordinary rate. Several thousand were written and produced during the period of Shakespeare's career.
- Plays were performed in a frequently changing repertoire: no play was performed more than once per week, companies performing a dozen or more plays in a season. The King's Men – Shakespeare's company – performed twenty plays, eight of them Shakespeare's, during the week-long celebration of the marriage of the Princess Elizabeth in 1613.

English Actor-Managers
The Long Tradition
Actor-managers have controlled theatre production in Britain since the Tudors. James Burbage (?–1597), William Shakespeare (1564–1616) and Edward Alleyn (1566–1626) were three stars of the Elizabethan theatre business. They were succeeded after the Restoration by entrepreneurs such as Davenant (1606–68) and John Rich (?1682–1761) who built Covent Garden on the proceeds of a single production. This tradition of actor-management continued through Macklin (1697–1797), Garrick (1717–79) and Foote (1721–77), to Kemble (1757–1823), Lucia Elizabeth Bartolozzi, known as 'Madam Vestris' (1797–1856), the Keans (early–mid-nineteenth century) and Henry Irving (1838–1905), and into the

Rehearsal Features of Elizabethan Drama

- Actors probably worked to commonly understood conventions of gesture and expression.
- Characters are portrayed according to convention. They are universal types. The actor makes no attempt to create 'individuals'.
- Rehearsal is brief and peremptory. Actors don't have time to invest in it because the London audience is too small to allow long runs of a single play.

- Exits, entrances and fight sequences are rehearsed, perhaps with a manager or lead actor. Actors only have their cue scripts, and must therefore listen for and speak to their cues.
- An actor must be able to dance, sing and fight. They are part of the theatre of total performance.
- Actors are in the open air, competing with street noise.
- The audience come to see bloody action and poetic rhetoric.

twentieth century with Beerbohm-Tree (1853–1917) and William Archer (1856–1924). The rise of the modern director occurred very late, and in response to the needs of ensemble production and the psychological interpretation of character.

An actor-manager is an entrepreneurial artist who stars in his own show. Kenneth Branagh is a modern example, as is Steven Berkoff, who says of his career as actor producer 'If I want to eat a sandwich, I have to build a restaurant.' Actor-managers are not the same as directors and it could be argued that the modern director didn't appear in the theatre until the 1880s. Actor-managers of the eighteenth and nineteenth centuries, like modern directors, took a variety of responsibilities for all aspects of production. This might range from the cutting, creating and shaping of the script, through the design and production of scenery and creating the stage picture in furniture and people, to paying the actors.

Actor-managers managed both the business of the company and the production. They also supervised the physical aspects of the production, often to a very high level, the actor-manager owning the entire means of production, sometimes including the theatre. The company sold the public not just the play or production, but the reputation of the actor-manager.

The actor-manager's relationship with the actor was strikingly different from that of most modern directors. The actor-manager neither interpreted the play nor the actor's role, and had no hand in the development of character. The independence of the actor within a company was possible because of the stage conventions, the character of the audience and the particular, distinct nature of the 'classical' actor.

The 'Classical' Actor – Acting Without Rehearsing
Acting between 1660 and the late nineteenth century was part of a single tradition. This is true in spite of the clear contrast in style between the classic restraint of the so-called 'teapot school' exemplified by John Philip Kemble, and the romantic 'freshness to nature' that was Edmund Kean and his imitators. Both schools observed certain 'classical' characteristics.

15

The 'classical' tradition was characterized by elocution, standardized gesture and heightened characterization. The acting style was designed to portray the tragedies and flaws of gods, aristocrats and latterly the middle class, who were flattered and elevated to these heights. Developed and refined during the eighteenth century, classical style gave the actor a set language of recognizable gestures, facial expressions and physical poses with which to show 'the passions'. The passions were externalized as physical shapes and patterns, always made with grace and beauty, however ugly the feeling. The actor spoke well and clearly, creating with his or her body graceful, expressive postures and pictures appropriate to the text. In the absence of text, a dumb show of set facial expressions might communicate to the audience the feelings flowing through the character.

Characters themselves were 'stock', and second-order actors usually pursued what was called a 'line of business', playing a single character type: the rake, the good mother, the juvenile lead, the innocent girl, the kind old man, and so on. There was a convention of 'possession of parts', and thus an actor could play a youthful role well into old age. Each of these types came with a toolkit of gestures, responses, clothes, props and deportment that made any discussion of interpretation with a director superfluous, indeed potentially detrimental to the clear portrayal of the type.

The stock actor, like the actor-manager, would have all the means to expertly portray a character and accurately express its emotional state without needing to observe either the physicality or the psychology of their character and without the intervention of a director. Actors usually learned from observing each other, techniques being handed down from generation to generation of professionals. They inherited their craft and were autonomous in the sense that they came to a production with their character type developed as a complete product, which they sold and resold throughout their professional lives.

Classical actors' characterizations were not necessarily stereotyped or banal. Interesting choices were possible within the convention of the type. Actors learned not by exploring possibilities in rehearsal but by rapidly creating roles within their type in front of the audience without benefit of rehearsal, and to a repertoire in which the plays might change nightly. Squire Bancroft (1846–1921) for example, played 346 parts in four years and Henry Irving played 428 different parts within the first two and a half years of his acting career. It is unlikely that either had much time for rehearsal.

David Garrick (1717–79)

Garrick was the most famous of actor-managers, and imposed 'company rules' on his actors concerning their behaviour, line-learning, punctuality and sobriety. He even fined miscreants! Exceptionally, Garrick was known to rehearse new productions in detail, holding sporadic rehearsals over a number of weeks. He would also take a production back into rehearsal and polish it while it was running. Unusually, he expected main and important actors who were already familiar with their roles, also to attend his rehearsals.

He began the rehearsal process by reading through with the whole company, commenting on the play and then describing the roles in detail. This suggests that he had what was at the time an eccentric interest in giving the whole company a common view of the play. Garrick was 'the great actor' and directed by demonstrating all the parts himself by acting them out, including female parts. Actors were expected to copy interpretations created by him. In effect he created a more innovative and individual 'type' – his own interpretation – but he expected the actor to go no further than to imitate him.

Victorian Theatre – the Development of Modern Rehearsal

The Growth of Mass Audiences

Until the nineteenth century, theatres played to relatively small communities. The theatre audience within these communities was pathetically small by modern standards: Elizabethan London had a population of 160,000, a high theatregoing audience of 20,000 and many open-air playhouses with a capacity of 2,000. To hold the interest of this relatively small theatregoing public, the companies changed bills daily and added poorly prepared new plays regularly. Modern rehearsal as we know it only became possible when companies

'Horror' after Henry Siddon's Practical Illustrations of Rhetorical Gestures (1822).

could be sure that they would get a return from their huge investment of two or three weeks' paid preparation. This return only became possible when single shows could attract large audiences and be sure of a long run of shows. Mass audiences only became possible during the mid-nineteenth century with industrialization, the growth of major cities and the rise of a large, concentrated ticket-buying population. The rise of a concentrated and relatively affluent population in major cities was accompanied by the development of the railway that linked them and, from the impresario's point of view, created one mass nationwide audience. At last long-running and well-tested West End productions could be seen in their original spectacular form in Manchester and Glasgow, since the development of road and rail allowed actor-managers to transport complete sets and whole companies round the country.

The Effect of Stage Lighting on Style and Staging

The first half of the nineteenth century was distinguished by its great acting 'stars' and by great technical innovation. Stage lighting had a fundamental affect upon stagecraft and its technical development greatly affected acting style and rehearsal practice.

Theatres were illuminated by daylight and flame until the nineteenth century. Although sophisticated contraptions augmented and intensified the relatively dim and uncontrollable candlelight in chandeliers and footlights, we can imagine the stench, heat and fire hazard of a packed theatre. Audience and actors alike were illuminated by a smoky orange light. This meant that the actor's physical and facial gestures had to be almost grotesque, otherwise they would not be big enough for the audience to be able to 'read' through the grime. The use of chandeliers on the English stage meant all the light fell on the apron so there was no natural stage 'blocking'; the actors had to stand in a line on the edge of the apron in order to be

17

Modern rehearsal of an eighteenth-century text. 'Truthful' playing plus an understanding of style has replaced notions of 'stock types' and 'lines of business'.

seen. Also the light, falling on audience and actor alike, made the theatre a single unified space containing both. It was therefore natural that actors should talk not to each other, but to the visible and usually vocal spectators.

Gas lighting, first used in 1817 at the Lyceum Theatre in London, created a much brighter light source. Still hot, smelly and unable to provide a beam, the brightness could be varied by regulating the gas supply. The quality of gaslight fundamentally affected acting style, its soft incandescence enhancing the style of the romantic stage. The next significant invention was limelight: a block of quicklime heated by an intense flame and installed in a handheld spotlight. This was first used at Covent Garden in 1837 and provided the first directional theatre lighting.

Henry Irving experimented with gas, lime and colour, holding complex rehearsals just for the light. These rehearsals needed no actors, but were attended by thirty gasmen and eight limelight operators. Irving was the first to darken the auditorium, leaving the actor isolated in a pool of stage light, cut off from the audience for the first time in theatre history. In the relative absence of an audience, for the first time actors needed a responsive 'ideal audience' – a director – to help them feel their way through the play and give, in rehearsal, the feedback that the actor formerly got in performance from the audience. As lighting transformed the audience from a bunch of rowdy spectators to a strong corporeal shadow, the actor's focus of attention turned from the auditorium to the stage – towards his fellow players. Actors began to play together rather than alone to the audience. Furthermore, the added brightness demanded a more natural 'observed' style, since more detail could be seen without the actors exaggerating their gestures. The new brightness now showed up the old-fashioned styles of scenery, costume, make-up and acting style as overblown, vulgar and garish.

Rehearsing 'Ensemble' – the Director's Role in the Meiningen Company

The Meiningen Company flourished during the final years of the nineteenth century. It was developed out of the Meiningen Court theatre by Georg II, Duke of Saxe Meiningen, and financed by him; his money allowed extended and detailed rehearsal. The Meiningen management was a partnership between Georg II and the director/ensemble coach Ludwig Chronegk (1837–91).

Stanislavski and Antoine, two directors who made seminal contributions to realistic theatre, were deeply influenced by the ensemble nature of Meiningen productions. These were quite distinct from the 'star productions' described above. The Meiningen Company conducted unusually extensive rehearsals – up to twenty-five rehearsals was not unusual. Furthermore, the sessions were long, bordering on the obsessive: a dress rehearsal of *The Maid of Orleans* lasted ten hours.

Chronegk coached the actors and set the famous crowd scenes whilst Georg's third wife, the actress Ellen Franz, coached character interpretation and Georg attended meticulously to the authenticity of the décor and costume. Georg eliminated 'lines of business' in favour of character interpretation, requiring expression rather than indication in acting, and a more 'natural' style. He abolished the convention of actors taking a round of applause after each dramatic exit, introduced appropriate music and effects to enhance realism and brought attention to detail in all respects to the production. His policy was to abolish the 'star' system, in favour of the ensemble. All actors, no matter how large or small their roles, attended all rehearsals.

Stanislavski thought Chronegk the genius of the group. Chronegk was something of a dictator: actors were summoned by hand-bell and fined if they infringed a long list of misdemeanors. Because they were part of an ensemble, major actors were also expected to play bit parts and walk-ons. When coaching crowds, mobs and choruses, Chronegk broke them into groups led by experienced actors called 'captains'. Players who had formerly been merely 'spear carriers' were encouraged to develop individual roles, the Duke encouraging attention to detail, for example by writing lines for them to speak while in the crowd.

The Rise of Literary Realism and Implications for Rehearsal

Realism is represented, for example, in Ibsen's play *Ghosts*, in Chekhov's plays, in Strindberg's defence of naturalism in the preface to *Miss Julie* and in some of Shaw's plays. Emile Zola's dramatization of his novel *Therese Raquin* (1873) is regarded as the first realistic play. Realism shows an interest in representation. It is interested in the inner lives of its characters and therefore lends itself to interpretation: choosing elements of motivation and characterization, a process that benefits from help from a modern director. It democratizes theatre writing in the sense that anyone's inner life is potentially as interesting as any king's or queen's, so for the first time theatre can deal with ordinary, unheroic, everyday life. Actors can observe this life in ordinary

Ensemble rehearsal in a modern context.

people, and realism as a style represented a move away from character 'types' and a gesture towards specifically observed settings, consistency of character and character development, use of ordinary as opposed to 'heightened' speech and modern problems as subject matter. Realism requires modern rehearsal which, with almost every aspect of theatre practice, changed radically in the wake of the new writing.

The Rise of the Director

The role of the director as an interpreting artist of the theatre is a twentieth-century idea. The constant evolution in the job descriptions of all theatre members is likely to continue and we can expect the nature of rehearsal and the work of the director to continue to be questioned.

The director as star-turn manager and entrepreneur has always been with us, but the conditions outlined above gave rise to the modern director, all of whom to some degree take on the following roles.

The Director as Ideal Audience

Extended rehearsal requires an articulate and communicating representative of the audience if it is going to remain focused on its purpose, which is to engage the audience. All directors have their individual way of feeding back to actors, and the feedback becomes, at best, a creative dialogue. This is Charles Marowitz observing Peter Brook:

> [The actors] want to please him, and this desire makes them exert themselves more than is usual for actors. Brook is cunning in his use of praise or admonishment, cold-bloodedly applying one or the other depending on what effects he thinks he may achieve ... Brook tends to work 'off' rather than 'with' people ... in the midst of a stew of contradictory suggestions, he is able to bring to the boil a clearly defined line of his own, but he seems first to need the stew.

(Marowitz, *The Act of Being*)

The Director as Mentor

Extended rehearsal became appropriate when a new psychological model of man was proposed by Freud and found simultaneous expression in Ibsen and Chekhov. In their plays, a character's motivation is often hidden, obscure or unconscious. Old rehearsal conventions of a dress, two blocking and a handful of general rehearsals were quite inadequate to uncover sub-textual psychology. Dozens of rehearsals were now necessary to tease out and interpret the roles. Stanislavski's early experiments were committed to discovering the 'inner truth' of characterization. He explored routes to character through the actor's personal 'affective' memory, adapted from the theories of the French experimental psychologist Ribot. Because truthfulness and commitment in art has moral overtones and is sometimes difficult and painful, the actor–director rehearsal relationship becomes highly personal and dependent on mutual trust. Although Stanislavski later abandoned and then moderated this approach, it was exported in 1923 to the United States where it flourished in the self-analytical culture of the time leading to the 'Method' approach of the New York Actor's Studio.

The Director as Puppeteer

The development of extended rehearsal and theatre technology created a space in which the many arts making a theatre production can be recombined and redefined. Edward Gordon Craig is the seminal example of the 'theatre artist'. He saw the director's job as combining the theatre arts through concepts of line, colour, rhythm and action into a single art. Craig's ideal director was an individual who controlled every action of the production, whose decisions could never be questioned. The actor was simply a factor in this combination, whose fragmenting and unstable ego could destroy it. Craig therefore proposed the *Übermarionette* or 'super puppet', which is a model of the actor with the physical, emotional and vocal self-mastery of a puppet. A contemporary exemplar of this directional attitude may be Robert Wilson, whose early work was evolved in rehearsal, using images, myths, icons and momentous décor, inspired by his vision but developed through combined arts collaboration. Wilson's solution to the actor problem was not the super actor but the non-actor, whose personal qualities, unselfconsciously given, supplied the element of raw nature he required to shape his work.

The Director as Teacher

Bertold Brecht held to the belief that education could change human nature and saw the task of the actor in the theatre as nothing less than to change the world. The director Giorgio Strehler said that Brecht had taught him 'the value of clarity and doubt': the company had to go beyond enacting a play, they had to believe in what it was saying. Brecht was an inclusive director, expecting the cast to contribute and eliciting comment even from visitors. Brecht always sought to moderate emotional empathy in the audience by creating a 'distancing' moment in which the audience returned from 'feeling' to 'thinking' mode, becoming once more aware of the social circumstances of the scene. His rehearsals began with his analysis of the play, including a discussion of its social insights. Actors were encouraged to work with the *Gestus*, the physicalization of their characters' relationships to their social circumstances. Story-telling, narrating the role in the past and in the third person, are techniques for 'demonstrating' a character. In spite of the plethora of theory, Brecht's rehearsals were very pragmatic – all suggestions to be demonstrated rather than discussed.

The Director as Interpreter

This major and controversial role demonstrates the rise of the director as a new collaborative artist, intervening between the writer, the actor and the audience. Should the director and the company work to fulfil the intentions of the writer or is the director entitled to interpret or reinterpret a text to meet the demands, needs and circumstances of the contemporary audience? Peter Sellars acknowledges that he has 'vandalized the classics'. He has a reputation in both opera and theatre for creating powerful metaphors by transposing the 'world of the play' into a language of visuals and action that disturbs and refreshes the audience's expectation. Jonathan Miller recognizes no obligation to a playwright once he's dead. The only rules, he says, 'are those of aesthetic consistency, formal elegancy and accuracy and artistic finesse, and need have no bearing on what the author actually meant'.

The Director as Auteur

Increasingly the artist-director consumes the role of the playwright, creating text out of improvisation. The work of Eugenio Barba is a clear example of this. His company, Odin Theatre, has a unique training process, which is, according to Barba, psycho-physiological. It uses acrobatics, circus skills, yoga and exercises derived from many cultures. Barba begins not with a vision but with 'fragments', which are analogous to a text draft. At the start of rehearsal Barba will present images, which the company will embellish with their own contributions, including text. The company create theme-based actions, which they refine and repeat using video. This is combined with music, visuals and movement as well as personal material, all gathered in rehearsal and shaped by Barba, as the theme and vision becomes clear.

Tadashi Suzuki's theatre derives from the dynamic between Eastern and Western culture. For five years until 1980, Suzuki trained actors in his own method in Togo, Japan. He synthesized Western acting techniques with the traditional Japanese acting traditions of *Noh* and *Kabuki* theatre, applying this new approach to classical Greek and Elizabethan texts. Actors learn, for example, the 'grammar of the feet'. Characters are triggered through skilled walking and footwork. The training stresses vocal and physical mastery. The words must emerge from the actor's physicalization, not from intellectualization. Suzuki often adapts Western classics – Greek tragedy, Shakespeare and Checkov, for example. These are sometimes played with Japanese and American actors speaking their own language. Suzuki creates adaptations and original texts, and resonates classical themes with contemporary issues.

2 ACTORS AND DIRECTORS – THE STATE OF THE ART

WHERE ARE WE GOING?

As a simple act of communication, theatre is timeless. As part of the entertainment industry it has had to respond, like all industry, to technological development and globalization.

Theatre, by definition a community art, has seen in two generations the disintegration of geographic communities and the growth on a global scale of electronic mass communities of interest. This has implications for the development and the nature of audiences. Just as in the nineteenth century the growth of cities and railways for the first time created mass national audiences, so global technology implies mass global audiences – cross-cultural, multi-ethnic and bound together not by location but by shared interest and taste.

New technology is creating the potential for new forms of performance, and artists are struggling to meet the challenge, sometimes using the old-fashioned art forms of film and television, just as film began by using the old-fashioned techniques of theatre. There are new opportunities for the actor, since the Internet itself is a potential performance platform. New technology may be a key to the future of theatre but, like all new forms, might demand a new type of actor.

This does not mean that technology is sweeping theatre away. Audiences fed on a diet of virtual experience might yearn more strongly for what is essentially human about the theatre. Theatre offers storytelling, live communication and intimate experience. The audience can put itself in the actor's hands, experiencing the essentially human, interactive aspects of traditional theatre. In a virtual world these opportunities may be needed more than ever.

There are significant implications for actors and directors. Perhaps the divisions of labour into actor and director are already redundant. Theatre is a collaborative art and it may be that this relationship will evolve to meet the new demands and opportunities. In the modern theatre, as in the whole field of employment, flexible, forward-looking workers who constantly keep abreast of new developments and update their training are likely to stay in work.

ARE ACTORS INSTRUMENTS OR ARTISTS?

The way actors behave in rehearsal is conditioned by their training. Should the actor be like a musical instrument waiting to be played? If so, the actor's job is to keep the instrument – their voice and body – in good condition, able to respond to the wide range of demands made on it by directors and play texts. On the other hand, should the actor behave as an artist? If so, the actor's job is to collaborate actively with other artists – directors, designers, musicians, and writers – and to bring their individual artistry to bear upon and make its mark upon the production. The former is craft training in the so-called 'conservatoire' tradition. The latter is informed by theories of teaching and learning, espoused by the university training environment.

Actors as Instruments

This is conservatoire training, and the name says much about how the actor is expected to behave. 'Conservatoire' suggests that actor training is analogous to the training of musicians. It implies methodical and progressive practice and performance under the direction of professional staff. Conservatoire actors are trained in the disciplines of voice, movement and acting. 'Acting' means improvisation, progressive acting exercises, text classes usually from the Western classical canon, and a continuous programme of scene studies and productions. However, in actor training the actor is 'the instrument', so development of the voice, the body and the imagination implies 'body and soul' personal development in the student. This requires regular and intensive classwork, since personal change is slow and difficult to sustain.

The purpose of conservatoire training is to produce an actor who can put 'the instrument' at the service of 'the work' – usually a play text. The measure of such actors is their ability to transform, become so flexible, and have such a wide vocal and physical vocabulary that all demands made by the director or the text can be met. The actor is dependent upon the text, upon the director and upon being offered a suitable role, in the same way as a classical musician depends on the composer, the conductor and the sheet of music. Conservatoire actor training seeks to replicate professional practice in its methods. It is responsive and reactive to the requirements of the commercial and the subsidized theatre.

Actors as Artists

Actor training in an university setting favours the training model of the fine artist over that of the musician. Fine artists studying painting, drawing or sculpture are asked to create and develop a portfolio of work, which is a testament to their imaginative originality and skill. The artist is given space and stimulus to grow in confidence and to acquire the skills necessary to their work. Training is more 'hands off' and encourages independent creativity. It values originality over virtuosity.

Fine art practice has an increasing influence on performing arts training. Performance art, in which artists use their own bodies as material, is a form that can come close to acting. Opportunities offered by the virtual and Internet stage have been taken up entirely by visual artists and not yet by actors. Theatre opportunities, which offer total creative control by the actor, occur in forms such as cabaret, puppetry and theatre clowning. Training is emerging to meet the demands of contemporary theatre. It seeks to create an artistically independent actor, a new model that up to now would have been regarded as unusual.

This training is like artist training in several ways. The actor acquires a toolbox of skills, often consisting of core skills plus options. A portfolio of work is often created through tape, video and the written record. While physical and vocal aptitude are required and valued, learning skills and independence are also valued as vital elements of professional competence. The training is eclectic, using a variety of methods, and there is usually a lot less of it. In accordance with university practice, there is a considerable amount of personal study and student-led study.

The actor's creative identity is always evident when devising, making individual performance, or working on traditional text. The actor is an active artist, able to function with or without writers, directors or casting agents.

DO WE REALLY NEED DIRECTORS?

Directors have been running the theatre since the end of the nineteenth century. Reviews, critical notices and academic attention increasingly focus on the work of the director, eclipsing those indispensable craftsmen and -women of the stage – the designers, actors and playwrights. The history of twentieth-century theatre is the history of 'guru' directors, yet the contribution they make is, of all the theatre artists, the most difficult to quantify. The secrecy of the rehearsal room makes it easy for the audience to endow directors with a power they don't really have. Career critics, whose meteoric rise took place at the same time as that of directors, have encouraged this, since it is easier to analyse and intellectualize the director's 'concept', than to put into words the non-verbal expression of the actor.

The director, absolute ruler in the rehearsal room, is impotent and ultimately redundant once the production moves to the stage. The axiom that good actors can elevate a mediocre director but a good director can't do the same for a bad actor is nearly true, and powerful though directors seem, we haven't always needed them. Although there have always been writer-managers, actor-managers and writer-actor-impresarios, the history of the modern director is remarkably short. At the turn of the century they were distinguishable from production managers by their function as pseudo-audience, easing the loneliness of actors destined to perform to shadows, mentoring them through the labyrinths of psychological parlour plays. Since that time the director has struggled to find a position in the creative process. Somewhere between the writer and the actor? Between the actor and the audience? The director's famous 'concept' at best sharpens and clarifies the text and at worst splashes an irrelevant ego all over the stage.

So do we really need directors? We obviously need someone to manage the production and create by some means a practical stage picture – a *metteur en scène* – but a designated actor or a stage manager could do this. Directors regard themselves as artists and a question should hang over the necessity for this extra intervention between the actor and the audience. How should the director relate to others artists in theatre-making, which is a uniquely collaborative art? Will the director be forced in the future to adapt and change to meet the changing demands not only of audiences but also of fellow artists – actors and designers – now better educated and more independent than ever before?

Managing Directors

Directors have conventionally assumed total responsibility for and total authority over the entire production process, defined in terms of their conception and vision. Artists are briefed by the director, and subsequently work to meet his or her requirements.

There are pre-rehearsal meetings with the designer, lighting designer, costume department and the production team. The designers present models and blueprints to the director, which once agreed, serve as production decisions. These decisions are taken very early in the process, often before the director meets the actors. The director may not meet the production team again until very late in the rehearsal process. The director has the same formal relationship to the actors as to the production team. He/she sets them objectives and tasks, and they do as they are told.

Conventional directors are characterized by the clarity and relative rigidity of their initial vision of the production. Their role is to hold the other artists to this vision, and to accept nothing less. They are essentially 'managing directors' and are differentiated by their management style, which might be anywhere on the spectrum from highly authoritarian to highly collaborative.

Collaborating Directors

Modern directors rarely come to rehearsal knowing everything, and even if they say they do, they are pretending! Their vision is always moderated by production practicalities. They will not be able to cast exactly to their vision; time and money will moderate some ideas; the world of the play will look different on the rehearsal floor than it did in theory, before the process started. These facts of life encourage some directors to a more collaborative approach in which the production concept evolves through rehearsal. Many modern directors are natural collaborators, and modern management style, which is team-orientated and favours delegation, is appropriate to efficient rehearsal management.

Collaborating directors prepare by defining what 'hooks' them into the play. These might be thematic, aesthetic or political factors, depending on the script. The director will be sufficiently clear to inspire vision in the company and production team. There will be a vision but it will be, so to speak, a 'draft' vision: open to revision through the input of the entire company.

The rehearsal process is usually transparent: the issues and obstacles are understood by all. The director has fewer options in the tactics he or she can employ in dealing with the actor. The director must facilitate and negotiate, rather than manipulate and command.

Meetings with the production team are brief, frequent and take place throughout the rehearsal process. Designs evolve and may change radically as the production grows.

Designers, managers and actors are seen as a team of collaborating artists co-ordinated, facilitated and led by the director. Designers are frequently asked to attend rehearsal, becoming part of the ongoing evolution of the production.

The director retains final responsibility for the production and takes all final decisions, but is also responsible for discovering and exploiting the entire resource of skill and talent in the company, not just those seen as useful to the initial concept.

Theatre Makers

It is unlikely that the director's role will become redundant in the theatre. There are many shows and plays that require the iron hand of the control freak we have come to know and love. However, other relationships are often more appropriate. Successful and effective collaborations between designers and directors, between actors and designers or between actors and musicians, which produce striking company style, are part of the contemporary scene. Small companies like to be directed by organized working actors who understand what it means to perform on stage. The actor-director is in ascendance. Indeed, the modern theatre practitioner is exactly that: actor, director, writer and designer; a complete theatre person. Collaborations exist between a range of skilled practitioners: actors, performers, designers, puppeteers, directors, acrobats, musicians, fine artists, performance artists, sculptors, theatre clowns, and jazz, opera and folk singers. The list is endless, and it is the creative collaboration between these practitioners with distinctive skills to offer that may point to the future for stage performance.

3 THE ACTOR/DIRECTOR RELATIONSHIP

REHEARSAL CULTURE

Great acting makes a public display of what is most private and intimate about being human. By contrast there is almost a fetishistic secrecy about the rehearsal process that helps create those great moments. There are a few exceptions. In the Globe Theatre in London, visiting parties of tourists might come across a company rehearsing on the open stage, and find themselves suddenly confronted by an actor in full flow, taking the opportunity to practise on the passing trade, but this is exceptional. The public is rarely allowed to observe the relationship between the director and actor.

In permanent companies, particularly if the uniqueness of the rehearsal process is part of the company profile, standard working practice will have developed from the company philosophy. Every company rapidly develops into a small society with its own laws and culture. These are established quickly and unconsciously early in the rehearsal process. Company culture develops in parallel with the production, and the director's management style is crucial to the process.

Unfortunately, company culture is often not apparent until its symptoms are beginning to emerge, and then if the culture is pernicious it is hard to change. Rehearsal culture directly affects the actor–director relationship because it determines whether actors will feel safe to extend themselves and take risks.

Company Culture and Company Practice

In permanent companies, the culture arises from the unique performing style of the company – the result of distinct working habits – for example, an ensemble company producing Shakespeare and the classics, in which all of the actors stay onstage for the entire performance and therefore attend all rehearsals, often behaving as chorus when not engaged in a scene.

Features of Good Company Culture

- Good timekeeping from the whole company, including the director.
- The company regularly reviews its achievements and assesses its tasks in the context of a planned process.
- A sense of serious intent at every level of rehearsal including games and play.
- Dissatisfaction with any but the highest quality of work and a willingness to redouble effort to achieve this.
- Actors regularly bring along prepared suggestions to try out in rehearsal.
- The company regard the production as their collective responsibility.
- Rehearsal is conducted in the spirit of mutual constructive criticism.
- The atmosphere in the rehearsal room is light and concentrated.

Actors have an additional skill: they are actor/musicians or actor/dancers, and conduct workshops with the company in consultation with the director.

On the other hand, a 'new writing' company, in which the early rehearsals workshop the major themes of the new production, will organize its rehearsals quite differently and will value different collaborations. Writer and director work closely to develop themes and characters appropriate to individuals in the company. There is then a break for four weeks or more during which the writer writes and the company research their characters. A conventional rehearsal process follows this.

RELATIONSHIP DYNAMICS

In performance, actors look for the moment when their character is completely exposed and transparent to the audience. Preparing for this in rehearsal creates a series of confidence crises, and confidence is the one thing a director cannot give the actor. Resisting the temptation to reassure, may be the most creative option for the director, since a confidence crisis in an actor with a genuine artistic temperament may indicate the quality of his or her work. They may have good reason to worry that their choices are not yet sufficiently bold or specific. Such a state is highly creative, though uncomfortable. Experienced actors may come to look for this discomfort as a trusted friend. Directors therefore have to find ways to work with the actor's state of doubt, 'holding' the discomfort rather than trying to cure it, which simply distracts from the job of doing the play. The director must find the most facilitating relationship, tone of voice, imagery and language. This is different for each actor. Some, for example, must be featherbedded with praise in order to hear any encouragement at all. Others will not be able to respect the director's judgement unless he or she adopts a critical, almost insulting attitude.

The director must find a different tone of voice for each actor.

This edgy, gently challenging dynamic is essential to the development of rehearsal. Uncreative relationships are chummy, conspiratorial and infused with false confidence, in which having a pleasant time together is more important than the quality of the show.

THE DIRECTOR'S MANY HATS

The director plays many roles in the course of a rehearsal, simultaneously planning the production process while responding to the creative needs of the company. For example:

- The director will act as *guardian of the space*, maintaining a safe rehearsal space in which actors can experiment, make mistakes and test decisions without having to suffer the consequences of failing in front of an audience.

- The director may serve as an *'ideal audience'*, super-sensitive, responding, reacting and bluntly communicating.
- The director might act as *provocateur*, goading the actor, exposing the half truths and lies, and stripping away the actor's everyday pretensions while preserving a creative, safe space in which the actor–observer relationship can be taken to its limits.
- The director *guides* the company through the rehearsal, serving as mentor when the creative process feels barren or blocked, or as midwife, giving shape and meaning to the actor's experiments and explorations, and encouraging and developing half-formed or tentative ideas, sometimes subconsciously expressed.
- The director is usually a *trainer*, setting the standards of success and achievement, planning the preparation programme and assessing progress.
- Directors *witness* the actor's struggles, triumphs and failures.

ISSUES OF TERRITORY

Exactly how does the director fit into the rehearsal ritual? As a passive audience substitute the answer is easy: the director sits out and

Placing the actors on the marked-out rehearsal floor (dir. Andrew Visnevski).

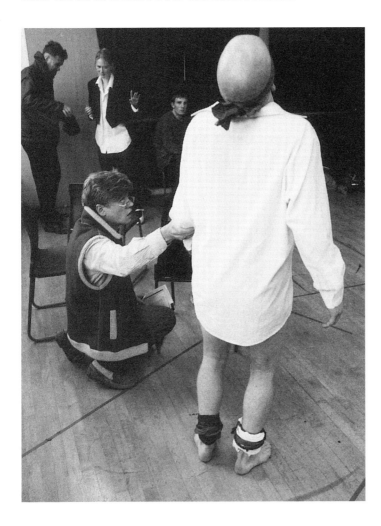

Hands-on direction.

shuts up, subsequently making helpful suggestions. Most directors take a much more robust view of their role, and this comes from the problem of communicating a suggestion without prescribing what the actor does. These are issues of territory between the director and the actor.

REHEARSAL ETIQUETTE

Should the director walk into the rehearsal space and demonstrate the notes he has just given the actor by doing the moves and reading the lines? The answer is almost certainly 'No'. Even if the director were a superbly accomplished actor, the proper route for the actor is to discover a personal solution to the problem, not to copy someone else. And yet time and again directors are seen unconsciously camping up the text to bemused actors in an attempt to demonstrate what they require. This case demonstrates the need for the director to maintain a distance from the actor, because the distance is the actor's creative working space. Squeeze it out and you leave a frustrated artist with no choice but to try to imitate your (usually bad) example. The director, however disposed to control, can never do more than hint, indicate the next step and be crystal clear when the result is not right.

In fact, judicious withdrawal often produces good results where the director's attempts to demonstrate have failed dismally. Actors often understand the task in their heads long before they can solve it. If the director lays a path and lets the actor discover the way through, the actor learns through self-discovery rather than through the imposition of ideas. Techniques such as taking the actor into your confidence and confessing you don't know how to solve the problem often produce spectacular results.

However, the point is for the actor and director not to play games, but to maintain a working relationship as equal partners and mature adults, finding an alliance in the common purpose of making the play. This is important since the director represents the audience to the actor, and when the time comes to perform, the actor will feel most free if the audience represents equal adults and not approving, disapproving or love-withdrawing parents, which is what the director can so easily become in rehearsal.

WHO OWNS THE SPACE?

This again raises the question of the of the creative distance between the actor and the

The loneliness of the long-distance director.

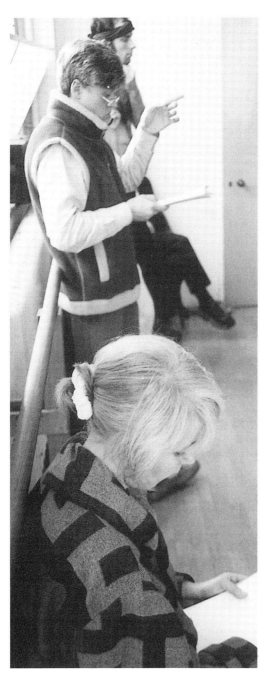

Note the position of the text: the director can see both the text and the action.

director. Directors take different attitudes to the rehearsal space, some rambling all over it and some never venturing onto it, staying discreetly behind their desk.

Some will have absolute respect for the actor's space and will not venture onto the stage. Others will get close and whisper in the actor's ear while he is speaking or move him gently round the stage. Others will talk to the actor in a level conversational tone while the actor is speaking, expecting the words to drop straight into his or her unconscious. These unorthodox techniques can work with some actors at a latish stage of rehearsal, while others are distracted and enraged at being interfered with while they are working.

FINDING A COMMON LANGUAGE

The director's job is to find a language that represents common ground on which actor and director can understand each other. The director cannot assume that the actors share his or her particular frame of reference. Actors are much more likely to nod and smile than to say that they don't understand what the director is saying. Directors have to test out the actor's comprehension. The instruction must not just inform, it must also move the actor. The director may use technical instruction, if the actor and director both understand a common technical language, such as that of Brecht or Grotowski, or technical terms of the 'method'. Imagery and analogy is always useful as a heightened, visual language. For example: film – 'You play a sort of Margaret Dumont to his Groucho'; cooking – 'Here you're beating it up and ... this is where you sling it into the pan'; music – 'Start small, like a single flute, here come the strings' or ' here you sound like a strong bass line'; and driving – 'Hold it in third for as long as you can, into top here, then slam on the brakes'.

4 THE HEART, MIND AND GUTS OF THE PRODUCTION

The modern director dreams up and drives forward the production. A good director is an effective leader and manager, has vision, and can make decisions and take responsibility for them, not knowing until the opening night if they will work. Directors must:

- love the piece they are working on;
- be level-headed in balancing all the vested interests against the needs of the production;
- have the courage to take uncomfortable decisions.

Competent directors have ability in all three areas, though for most there is a balance of strengths and weaknesses.

THE 'HEART' OF THE PRODUCTION IS VISION

Before the company starts to rehearse, the director is alone with the idea of the production. Already engaged by the text or scenario, the director uses this time to find a way to inspire the whole company – the production team as well as the cast. A strong sense of the 'world' and 'style' of the production comes from the director's initial research, but vision is not just a collection of ideas and arguments: vision means giving shape to these things and communicating them passionately. It is very enjoyable, because you are doing what you find irresistible, playing with ideas without being burdened (yet!) by the practical problems of staging them. These irrational explorations produce the rationale for your production.

Directors develop a way of working that is personal to them, but always based on the need to solve practical problems quickly, with correct priorities and in the right order. Every production concept is original and particular to the individual director, and this chapter also is a personal approach, not a set of laws. It must be adapted according to the demands of the production and the director's personal approach.

Starting Out

Start by re-reading the play or, if you don't have a play, finish rewriting the treatment. It has already seduced you. How did that happen? It doesn't have to grab you or be instantly gratifying. Very difficult and dense plays are sometimes irritatingly intriguing at first glance. On re-reading, focus on the detail, going over and over the knots in the piece: the moments that fill you with ideas and images, or don't add up; are immediately transparent, or are incongruous. Read these moments over and over, and allow

 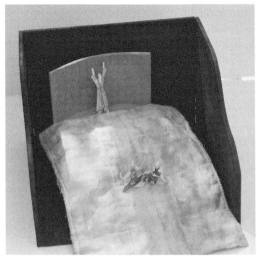

Arabian Nights *comprises rostra with a little cyclorama (designed by Rebecca Jannoway). The actors must tumble around the set and therefore need the rostra from the start of the rehearsal. Note the black box representing the theatre space and the figures to scale.*

Arabian Nights. *The set is a huge duvet that creates the desert, a bed, costume and the sea.*

BELOW: **Arabian Nights**. *The production (dir. John Perry).*

your imagination to take you through the text to somewhere else. Nothing at this stage is logical or methodical, but this is where you begin to 'envision' the production. You need to be immersed in the text, letting it take you into music, painting, sculpture, other cultures, novels, anything that will stimulate your response to it in a sensuous or visceral way. At the same time as responding to it, you will wish to test it. 'Responding' is a yielding, emotional action, but 'testing' is active and intellectually rigorous. Test moments in the text using research, which might involve the social and political context of the writing, the life of the writer, original documents. You will discover the writer's angle on their material and a political or historical viewpoint may become clear. You may agree with this or disagree, or develop interesting angles of your own. You may even abandon the play at this point if it seems that you cannot live in its world. If you stay with it, a concept will arise in your imagination, which is your strongly felt idea of the world of the play.

The Concept and the Text

The concept should arise from the text and not be imposed upon it. You must therefore test your concept against the entire text in all its detail, so this is where you read the whole text many times, marking its conformity or deviance from the concept, and developing the concept. To impose an idea on a play with scant reference to the actual text is a form of bowdlerization. The bowdlerizers historically are worried that we, the audience, might be morally corrupted by the play. They therefore 'fix' the text to serve their own social or political needs. Shakespeare is traditionally a victim of this propaganda: the Victorians used to fix Shakespeare to give the plays optimistic endings and ensure that the morally good always triumphed over evil. Today it is sometimes said, for example, that *The Taming of the Shrew* would be impossible to produce unless adapted for a modern audience. Bowdlerizing is always ethically and artistically highly questionable. If you have your own view of the world, write your own play but don't be a parasite on another artist's vision.

Devising is entirely another matter. You are entitled to use lumps of Shakespeare and gobbets of other things and mix them up in any way you like. The reworking and retelling of stories has a long and honourable history – Shakespeare and Chaucer did it all the time. If devising, test how big your concept can make the devising idea by brainstorming the possibilities of the concept within the devising idea. Again, the concept must be consistent with the devising idea, otherwise you will be trying to reconcile complications and irrelevancies late in the process.

The last stage in developing your vision is to apply it thoroughly to all of the arts of the theatre, to the stage space, to the set that defines the space, to the texture and colours of the surfaces, the costumes, to live or electronic sound, and so on. All of the theatre arts combine within your concept. This may be the time to include other artists such as the designer, lighting designer, musical director, stage manager and production manager, if you have them. Consider how you might relate to them: will they be part of the rehearsal, developing their ideas by coming into rehearsals, or will you brief them and agree the task during a few production meetings?

THE 'MIND' OF THE PRODUCTION IS PLANNING

If vision is the heart of the production, then planning is its head. Directing is both an art and a business, and planning is the business end of directing. It is important to plan ahead throughout the rehearsal process. However inconvenient it feels to stop rehearsing in order to plan, time is always saved by doing this.

A Production-Planning Sequence

1. Set down on a chart the date of the opening night, and the date of the 'technical and dress rehearsal'. Write them down and mark them as deadlines.

2. Mark your first rehearsal or production meeting. Mark off the days in between.

3. List whatever technical skills your concept requires of the actors: multiple characters, dressing onstage, greeting and interacting with the audience, farce skills, accent skills, song, dance and all interaction between the cast and stage technology. Begin these technical rehearsals early in the process. Allow time at the start to get the actors to the point where they can practise skills together when you aren't around. Bear in mind that you might want to make time for skills practice throughout the rehearsal.

4. Assess the technicalities of the production. If you are lucky enough to have a designer, a stage manager or even a production team as part of your company, assess and discuss with them what relationship is appropriate to the production:

   • If the set and props are 'practical' – that is, handled by the actors – they, or substitutes, will be needed early.

   • It may be appropriate for the designer or production team to attend rehearsals, if the production concept is 'integrated' and the design concept is evolving through the rehearsal period.

   • In a standard rehearsal situation, however, the director briefs the designer, discusses and agrees the model of the set with the designer, then meets the stage manager or production manager to agree the budget priorities and agree deadlines for building the set, for obtaining props, costumes and so on.

5. Given the world of the play, assess the improvisations you need, to give the actors a sense of the style of the play. Allow time for this.

6. Weigh the text (a kilogram is more than enough for any audience!). Do you want to cut it? If so, don't let the cast get attached to the bits you want out. Cut early, preferably at a very early rehearsal.

7. Assess how long it will take you to work the scenes.

8. Mark all the production landmarks. When do you want the cast 'off the book', i.e. playing together confidently without the text in their hands? When do you want the routines/songs performable? When do you want the practical props, costume and set elements?

9. Remind yourself that nothing is ever quite right in the theatre. The cast is never quite right, there's never enough money, and it's the wrong theatre and possibly the wrong play. Never mind. Do it anyway, but plan for the obstacles!

10. Now mark all of the above as deadlines on your chart. When will you have finished improvising? Working scenes? Learning lines? Developing character? Running scenes together? When is your first run-through? Do you want a photocall?

11. Remember that nothing stays the same in the theatre. You will change your schedule, improvise, make do and encounter the unexpected. Don't give your schedule to the cast, but consult and revise it as you make out your weekly targets.

THE 'GUTS' OF THE PRODUCTION IS DECISION-TAKING

Directors have to have guts, that is, the will to take clear but sometimes difficult and unpopular decisions. It is the lonely part of the job, because advice from company members is usually not very objective and involves their own vested interests, so whatever discussions take place, even the most inclusive director has to take the final decision alone. It is important that the company sees that the director is prepared to take responsibility for decisions: this allows everybody else to relax and get on with their job. Being decisive doesn't mean being quick or impulsive. In fact, timing – choosing the right time and the right way to say difficult things – is an important directorial skill because the language and currency of rehearsal is emotion. This means that if you say things in the wrong order, or in a way that could be misconstrued or misunderstood, then they probably will be and you will have problems in addition to the ones you started with.

Rehearsal often feels messy or totally blocked. Sometimes the director's job is to stay with the difficulty and stay in the mess, rather than try to make the atmosphere more comfortable. Sometimes if you stay with a problem, solving it will solve the play, but you need leadership qualities to do this. When and whether to do these things can only be learned through the trial and error of experience.

REHEARSAL LANDMARKS

Casting and Auditioning

It is sometimes said that casting is the most important decision that the director has to make. This is not true, but mistakes made at this stage will certainly affect the entire rehearsal period and fundamentally effect the production, so casting is a delicate matter for the director. The process involves the director asking him- or herself a series of questions and

'*Making the text physical', a rehearsal moment from* Up and Under *(dir. Robert Horwell).*

answering as honestly as possible. The final choice is often the director's alone.

Can the actor play the role just as they are, with no work or transformation? Although it is rarely possible to cast a company of clones from photographs, this 'type casting' is often used because it is thought to be safe. A type-cast company will give you an entirely predictable rehearsal process and probably a dreary show.

Directors are sometimes more ambitious than this and will ask whether the actor has the potential to fulfil the role, or will bring something new to it, within the production concept. They are looking not for a finished product, but for a quality, a tone and a presence. They will have to decide whether it's possible to achieve what is necessary in the limited rehearsal period. This begs the question 'Can the actor take direction?' The director tests this at audition.

Will the actor fit in with/enhance the company style, working methods and the production team? The importance of this depends on circumstances, since it's not necessary to like the people you work with. However, if the company is going to spend six months touring in a van, if the theme is personal or intimate, if ensemble work is required, or if the company must devise the show, then compatibility is an important consideration.

The Phases of the Rehearsal Process

The overall rehearsal can be broken down into three phases:

1. The early phase, in which the world of the play and the acting style is explored. Simultaneously the culture of the rehearsal room, the professional relationships between the actors and between them and the director is established. Themes and concepts are explored through discussion and exercises, and the play or scenario may be read and workshopped a number of times. The different approaches to workshops and exercises are discussed in Part 3 and a description of the conventional rehearsal process can be found in Chapter 9, on text.

2. The middle phase of rehearsal deepens and intensifies the process, the director working with a few actors at a time, and occasionally calling the company. Actors can work alone during this period and Chapter 12 suggests practical possibilities for actors working alone, preparing to work with the director or researching character and relationship possibilities. During this phase the full creative potential of the piece is explored. At the same time decisions 'set' what the director regards as the most effective rehearsal choices. The play may be 'blocked', and energy drops as it is diverted into line learning. At the end of the middle phase, technical issues start to intrude upon the process.

3. In the final phase the actors are off the book and the scenes are being run together. The director begins to call regular whole company rehearsals and the 'big picture' discussed during Phase 1 is reawakened in the company. Rehearsals concentrate on seasoning the playing, retaining the 'life' in each scene, communicating in the space and with the audience, and developing shape and rhythm in the whole piece.

Dress and Technical Rehearsals

This is usually the point at which the technical arts of costume, props, light and set are integrated with the actor's stage action. This is done in a matter of hours, and is a risky strategy in spite of the phenomenal speed with which the whole company – actors and technicians – are able to construct the piece. 'Tech-ing' at the last minute is the cheapest way of getting the show on, though many directors, given the choice would prefer to allow technicians and actors to play together earlier in the rehearsal. Given the pressure of a conventional technical and dress

A Possible Audition Process

Audition Task or Test	Questions from the Director
The actor reads a prepared two-minute audition speech – either 'classical' (written pre-1900) or 'modern' (post-1900)	• Has the auditionee professionally prepared and presented the pieces? • Do they make 'human' choices in performance or do they prefer tricks? • Do they capture the style and the world of the play? • Have they actually read the play? • Are they physically and vocally equipped for classical text? • Are you enthralled? Engaged? Interested?
The director redirects a moment in the audition speech	• Do you and the actor communicate well? • Does the actor understand your suggestions? • Will they try out your suggestions? • When they repeat the moment, is it different? • Is it more what you want?
The director gives the actor an unprepared piece to read	• Can the auditionee sight-read? • Does the actor apologize or otherwise break the flow if they make a mistake, or do they make the piece work? • Are they communicating while they read? • Is the reading sensitive or mechanical?
The actor is asked to read for the play, without preparation	• If this is not a new play, have they troubled to read it before the audition? • Do they bring the part to life? • Are they at ease with the world of the play? • Can you see the character in the actor?
The director redirects unprepared work	• Does the auditionee co-operate? • Are they flexible? • Are they prepared to try out ideas?
The director plays games with a group of auditionees	• Does the auditionee join in? • Can they relax with the game? • Do they have a playful energy? • Do they have a go?

continued overleaf

A Possible Audition Process *continued*

Audition Task or Test	Questions from the Director
A small group of auditionees are asked to prepare and present a piece of work in five minutes	• Can the auditionee relax with the group? • Can he/she balance talking and listening? • Can he/she let someone else take control? • Do they create a useful role for themselves? • Is the auditionee a talker or a doer? • Are they happy to show unfinished or messy work?
Interview	• Are you getting the real person or a performance? • Do you believe their answers? • Do they have the background, experience, skills and qualities that the production needs? • Could you work with this person?

run, the director should work to keep the period as tension free as possible.

The technical run is for the technicians, not the actors. Actors should be asked to be patient, relax and be ready to be called to the stage. This rehearsal is best taken by the stage manager, who should have a complete prompt copy with all technical cues, lighting cues, and complicated technical manoeuvres like set changes, flying and quick costume changes marked. The technical cues are now rehearsed in sequence, and the technicians and actors involved in technical matters are rehearsed until they are confident. The director will run the 'tech' if there is no stage manager, but will wish to be present anyway because many new ideas and decisions will present themselves as the production technicalities come together with the action. If there is no costume parade the director might want to check costume and make-up with the lighting. Techs are often long, and some are made over-long by the director's lack of preparation. Conventional techs cannot be run properly without an absolutely comprehensive technical cue sheet.

The dress run is where the technical and acting elements of the show are played at performance pace. It is often a dreadful experience for the director, because the acting seems to have died under the weight of technical notes, which the actors are 'playing'. The director must on no account stop the run because the whole company is experiencing – however haltingly – the rhythm, pace, fluidity and unity of the whole piece. The company must also learn to carry the show on its own without support, whatever happens. The director should take notes for the actors and technicians by drawing two columns, and give notes judiciously after the run. Give a fifteen-minute break and ring all notes that it would be unhelpful or destructive to give at this stage; find another occasion to give them. Be encouraging and upbeat without underplaying the work still to be done. The company needs to improve right through the technical runs and early performances, so they mustn't be demoralized at this stage. If you discover you have a turkey on your hands, the time to say so is about a month after the finish of the run, not at the dress rehearsal.

Sample Plan – *Caucasian Chalk Circle* by Berthold Brecht, dir. John Perry, 1996

Description
- A large-scale 'epic' play based on a parable.
- An 'anchor' role in each half (Grusha and Azdak) with a multiplicity of supporting parts requiring doubling and multiple roles.
- Style: narrative, storytelling, 'open' theatre style, where the actor's process, costuming and preparation is not hidden from the audience.
- The play features narrative, movement and song.

Production Choices
- Julian Dawes's score for percussion and piano was used, which requires the actors to both play and perform.
- Characters were to be strong, easily identifiable 'types'. No attempt was made to create a community of Caucasian people, rather a community of disparate types: middle-class Lancastrians, Chinese Mandarins, First World War soldiers and Russian intellectuals.
- Costumes and props entirely to support the 'type' – no attempt at consistency.
- It was possible to use a large chorus as courtiers, plaintiffs, refugees and peasants.

Technical Tasks
- Unless the actors know exactly where to be on the stage, the production will be a mess, so a pattern is worked out before the first rehearsal, showing the actors where to stand when not performing or playing.
- A list of actor/musicians is worked out to co-ordinate the acting and playing for the whole score. Actors know at the first rehearsal what part of the score is their responsibility.

- Songs, individual and chorus, are allocated.
- Songs and percussion playing is scheduled intensively early in rehearsal so that the actors have enough information to take on the tasks by mid-rehearsal.

Ideal Production Plan (5 weeks)
Week 1
- Read through the play and agree cuts. Designers describe set and visual concept. Discuss why we are doing it.
- Company gets a prepared scene plan showing who is available to play music at every stage of the play. Test the practicality of actor and musician sequencing.
- Rehearse songs and dances every day.
- Rehearse as a company, not as cast. Company tells the story of a scene then plays it out, sometimes using the book, sometimes improvising. The emphasis is on 'showing the story' to each other.

Week 2
- The company is onstage at all times. Stage managers mark up the stage area on the rehearsal room. Mark through the whole play, going from acting to music to observing. Company take notes so everyone knows where they are at every moment in the play.
- Detailed work on scenes using 'work rhythms' in the play – washing, spinning, soldiering and cooking. Use work rhythms to expose inner states.
- Start character work with the whole company, working for a company style. Distinguish characters and two-dimensional 'types'.

continued overleaf

Sample Plan *continued*

Week 3
- Intensely rehearsing scenes in pairs and groups. Actors rehearse alone when not needed.
- Music rehearsals simultaneously.
- Designers and production team observing rehearsal.
- Two workshops in which the actors develop the skills of 'being' and 'showing' their characters.

Week 4
- Intensely rehearsing scenes in pairs and groups.
- Groups of actors rehearse without the director when not needed.

- Also practise crowd and chorus scenes.

Week 5
- Rehearsing scene groups with music.
- Carefully plot a slow run with costume changes, props and musical instruments.
- A series of runs, in slow motion, silent run (music and songs the only sound), straight runs with notes.
- Technical run. Make photographers brief, check programme with cast.
- Dress and tech with photographer taking photos during run.
- Full dress run.

Notes for Up and Under *given with the level of energy the production requires.*

RECORDING REHEARSALS

Taking and Giving Notes

Acting is the most ephemeral of all the arts. No sooner has the actor created a moment of action than it has vanished, and the observer – the director in the case of rehearsal – must somehow recollect the moment and give the actor useful feedback. This is called giving notes.

Taking notes is a personal skill, refined by practice. It is impossible to give a formula for note-taking because it is so particular to the director. The director has to watch the action while making a mark or scribbling one or two words to remind him or her that something happened that needs comment, work or both. Some directors bury their head in their script, seeming just to listen to the actor. They will miss most of what's going on.

Notes on Note-Taking

- Begin by rehearsing in memory-size chunks, usually single scenes, breaking up big scenes into 'units'.

Taking notes (dir. Robert Horwell).

BELOW: *Director and stage manager taking notes during a run.*

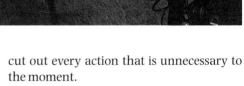

- When making notes write one or two words of the text to remind you of the specific moment that provoked you to comment. You will have no time to do more than indicate the note with a few words. You need to develop the skill of 'triggering' the thought in your memory by using a phrase or a couple of words.
- As you rehearse the play in larger pieces you will have more time to reflect. Tell the actors everything you write down. Sometimes the note feels clumsy or too personal, but it is important to find a way to expose every response immediately to the actor, otherwise you get into the habit of shelving problems and the actors will stop trusting you: there's no time for this.
- Respond like a rowdy audience. 'I can't hear!'; 'I don't understand you!'; and 'I don't understand the story at this point!' are simple comments and therefore very useful feedback to the actor, who doesn't have to translate esoteric claptrap into practical advice.
- Try to spot everything the actor does that is superfluous to the task. The actor may be doing too much or trying too hard, through a lack of confidence. Encourage the actor to cut out every action that is unnecessary to the moment.
- Directors sometimes ignore actors who are working well. Make an effort to respond to good work. Comment on everything the actor does that is good or (especially) nearly good. The director's job is to 'midwife' the

43

actor – to help give birth to vestigial or nearly formed moments.

- Sometimes a moment simply doesn't work: say so. Share responsibility with the actor. Use 'we' a lot in your notes. Privately look at the moments preceding or surrounding the difficulty.

The standard way to take notes is chronologically, but there are other ways. Sometimes, draw a series of columns and write 'action' (meaning the story) and 'tech', 'voice', 'style' and 'character' as the column headings. This will draw your attention to areas of the production that you might be neglecting. And sometimes write the actors' names down and take some specific notes for each of them as you watch the scene. Often the small parts get left out and a minor role can go through a whole rehearsal process without getting a note from the director.

Giving Notes

Note-giving is a major part of rehearsal culture. Principles remain the same, however many actors you are working with. If you are giving notes to the company, use the occasion to briefly review working patterns, the state of the production schedule and forthcoming tasks.

- Allow yourself and the actors a moment to settle down to emphasize that the 'doing' phase of rehearsal has finished and reflection has started.
- Wait until all of the actors are ready. It is important that actors hear each other's notes.

 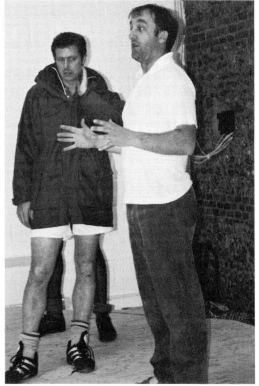

Notes – the director onstage and in the action.

- Encourage dialogue. Actors should feel free to respond to notes. Notes are a professional conversation, not a series of instructions.
- Strike out the notes in your book as you go. There will be scribbles and notes all over the page. Deal with every mark. Make sure you've dealt with everything on the page before moving on.
- Be brief, but make sure the actor has understood what you have said.
- Make it clear, if necessary, that you expect actors to write down your notes. Notes are to help the actor work alone, and should have had a palpable effect on performance by next rehearsal.
- Give a combination of specific notes to individuals, and general notes that deal with issues applicable to everyone.
- Inexperienced actors are inclined to 'play' notes. Often you give a note and the actor gives you a sort of wooden caricature of it the next time they play that moment. The actor has understood the note but not yet integrated the idea, and is showing you that that they heard what you said. It needs more practice to 'play the note in'. It is useless and sometimes destructive to give actors last-minute notes, if they are inclined to 'play' them.

RECORDING THE BLOCKING AND STAGE PICTURE

If a stage manager can be spared for the rehearsal room they will create a prompt copy and record rehearsal decisions in pencil so that you can alter and adjust as the rehearsal develops. A prompt copy is a play text interleaved with blank paper on which the blocking and effects are recorded (see page 46). Later the lighting, sound and stage effect cues are marked on the script and will be used to run the show. You will not always have the stage manager to hand, so it is useful to be able to mark the prompt copy yourself so that you can record rehearsal decisions.

BLOCKING

The director uses standard terms when 'blocking' actors, that is, moving them around the stage. The stage is divided into nine areas for this, as shown below. You may have to take a blocking rehearsal, though many directors prefer to allow the stage picture to emerge in an organic way from the onstage action. This is very good and invariably feels more natural to the actor, but does not always work for the audience. You will find that crowd scenes, all highly technical scenes, chorus scenes and especially farce, absolutely need blocking rehearsals. The grid in the diagram allows you to move the actor around the stage: upstage is the back of the stage and downstage is the front. If you say 'go upstage', the actor will walk to the back of the stage. If you say 'go upstage of the chair' the actor will stand behind the chair. An actor who upstages another sends them, in the audience's mind, to the back of the stage. While you do this, the stage manager is recording the moves in the prompt copy. Blocking is discussed further in Chapter 9.

The Areas of the Stage for Blocking

Up stage right (USR)	Up centre (UC)	Up stage left (USL)
Centre stage right (CSR)	Centre stage (CS)	Centre stage left (CSL)
Down stage right (DSR)	Down stage centre (DSR)	Down stage left (DSR)

The Stage Manager takes a script to pieces and pastes each page to a strip of A4 paper. Each pasted page is interleaved with a blank A4 sheet. The interleaved pages are placed in a ring binder and this is called the Prompt Copy. It is used by the member of the stage management team attending rehearsal and includes all cues for:

- Blocking
- Use of props and set
- Flying
- Lighting
- Sound cues

The illustration shows how a page might be marked. Lighting and sound cues are marked 'Standby' or S/B about half a page before 'Go', which is the actual cue. 'Go' would be marked in green, 'Standby' in red.

Cue Keys

S/B	Standby
LXQ	Lighting cue
SQ	Sound Cue
vis	Visual cue
FlyQ	Flying cue
F/S or Limes	Follow spot
M/D	Musical Director

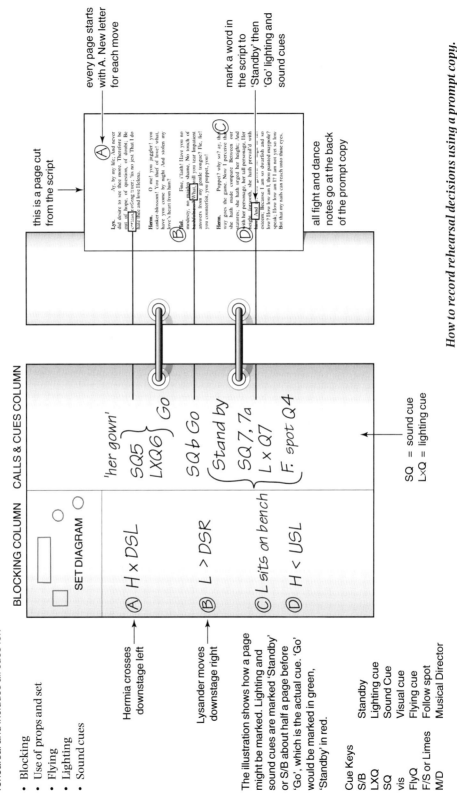

Hermia crosses downstage left

Lysander moves downstage right

every page starts with A. New letter for each move

this is a page cut from the script

mark a word in the script to 'Standby' then 'Go' lighting and sound cues

all fight and dance notes go at the back of the prompt copy

BLOCKING COLUMN   CALLS & CUES COLUMN

SET DIAGRAM

Ⓐ H x DSL

Ⓑ L > DSR

Ⓒ L sits on bench

Ⓓ H < USL

'her gown'
SQ5
LXQ6 } Go

SQ4 Go

Stand by
SQ7,7a
L x Q7
F. spot Q4

SQ = sound cue
LxQ = lighting cue

How to record rehearsal decisions using a prompt copy.

5 THE PERSPECTIVE OF THE PRODUCTION TEAM

THE PRODUCTION MANAGER

The production manager manages the entire technical team, ensuring that each person has the physical, financial and time resources to do their job. The budget is also the production manager's job. Production managers usually began as stage managers or lighting designers and sometimes double in one of these roles.

STAGE MANAGEMENT

The company will have a stage manager or, if large enough, a team consisting of the manager, a deputy and two assistants. During rehearsals the deputy (DSM) is in rehearsal, making the prompt copy and communicating changes from the rehearsal floor to the technical team. The DSM will be in the prompt corner, prompting and cueing the sound, lights and flying – running the show from the stage. The assistants (ASMs) will be making and getting props and attending rehearsal as required. They may organize props and scene changes, and they run the lights and sound during the show. The team is managed by the stage manager, and the whole team looks after the director and actors during rehearsal.

DESIGNER

The designer is often closest to the director and there are many successful director/designer teams and companies. The relationships and working patterns between the two vary widely. The designer may be asked to create a physical world in response to the director's ideas, but more usually there is an evolving dialogue extending well into the rehearsal period, in which the décor develops as the production grows through rehearsal. Although obviously shape, style, colour and texture are all vital to the success of the design, the designer should be especially concerned about the director's use of space. It is important to 'mock up' the space by marking in on the rehearsal floor as soon as possible. The space needs to feel dynamic and to encourage rather than obstruct the actors' free movement on it.

The designer is the key player in the production process. Not only does the design spring directly from the director's concept, but all technical aspects of the production – props, costume, sound and lights – depend and wait upon the designer's vision. Stage designers, like directors, can be collaborators or tyrants. Either approach can work effectively so long as the relationship between the designer and the production manager remains sweet.

PRODUCTION TEAM

The lighting designer is often also the production manager. This is so because the lighting designer's work takes on a consuming intensity very late in the production process and he/she is therefore free during most of the rehearsal process to devote time to management. The sound technician often doubles as the chief electrician and as such is responsible for reading the sound and lighting plans and creating an electrical plot, which will supply power where it is needed.

The costume team usually consists of a designer and assistants. They will take measurements early in the rehearsal process, discuss design with the stage designer, who will have an overview of the design concept, then make or hire what is necessary.

The stage carpenter builds the set, and sometimes doubles as the Flyman, designing and supervising the flying, if required.

HOW THEY PUT THE SHOW TOGETHER – PRODUCTION WEEK

A standard 'Get In' or 'Fit Up' involves putting every technical element of the production in place, ready for the tech and dress runs. The director and actors are rehearsing somewhere else while this is happening. The timescale of Get Ins varies according to the complexity of the show and its circumstances: the technical run of a West End musical might take a week; a tour would take a standard week to get into a suitable theatre, hired to rehearse the Get In, then a day to refit into its various venues. The work pattern in a standard six-day Get In is shown below.

Monday Carpenters on stage. They must complete the floor work and begin set-building. If they are slow, everyone else falls behind. Final costume fittings.
Tuesday Rig the lights. Carpenters work on. Where the set is built, scene painters begin finishing work under the direction of the set designer. The painters often work overnight when everyone else has gone home.

Wednesday Chief electrician fits up circuits to meet the plans of the lighting and sound designers.
Thursday The lighting designer now needs about eight hours of darkness to focus the lights. Others plan their work around this time.
Friday Fit the sound rig, finish lighting. Designers, stage managers and carpenters finishing. In the evening, plot lights with or without the director.
Saturday Director and actors arrive. Costume parade. Start the tech run.

PRODUCTION MEETINGS

A production meeting takes place every week between the director and the technical team. Ideally the entire staff should be present, but this isn't always possible. All meetings are chaired by the production manager and are minuted and distributed to all, including those in the team not present. This is important because it records the process by which the production manager keeps the production to schedule and within budget. The first meeting, often held before the director has begun to rehearse the actors, is vitally important because the production is explained to the technical team. Everyone must be present. The director describes the ideas that underpin the production and the designers add their ideas in terms of design, including the physical space, colour, texture, props, light, sound and costume. The discussion is usually very practical, turning ideas into a series of tasks and assessing the possibilities in terms of time and resources. The team will assess the consistency of all the production ideas and the production manager will assess the costs.

OPPOSITE PAGE:
Production meeting (production manager Di Stedman).

ABOVE: *At the first production meeting, the designer presents the 3D model.*
RIGHT: *The stage carpenter at work.*

There is sometimes a difficult meeting between the director, designer and the production manager if the latter's rough costing of the production comes well over budget. The designer has usually been working with the director and this is a test of whether the team can move creatively through obstacles and adjust the ideas without compromising the idea.

Subsequent meetings are best held weekly, in order to review the concept in the light of rehearsals and to check the budget. Production panics frequently override production meetings, though again, it often pays dividends to stop and do the planning.

PART TWO

REHEARSAL APPROACHES
FOR DIRECTORS

T here is no single way to put on a play, so the best way to plan a rehearsal is to start from first principles. What is the world of the play? What sort of community inhabits that world? What is the relationship between the community on stage and the community in the auditorium? Should we break or observe stage conventions? A fresh approach to the rehearsal process develops each time these questions are answered, and a plan can develop in which the world of the rehearsal room reflects the world of the play.

The following chapters therefore deal with principles of rehearsal practice, supported by examples, rather than formulae. Four approaches are explored: games, improvisation, devising and text. The chapters examine the relevance of each approach to rehearsal planning and the role of each on the creative process.

Exercises are suggested where appropriate. Rather than slavishly repeating them, it is more important that the reader understands the underlying principles of how to put an exercise together. Then it is possible to tailor games, improvisations and rehearsal exercises to serve a specific need, to work with a specific rehearsal problem.

Rehearsal plans should be simple, direct and flexible, which means they should have clear objectives that everyone can understand, they should address specific issues and there should be plenty of opportunity to adapt, develop or throw out the whole plan should the actual rehearsal situation call for it.

6 GAMES

PLAY AND THE THEATRE

It is no accident that we do a 'play', and that we 'play' a part, or a character. The theatre event, with its rituals, roles, unspoken rules and infinite strategic variation is essentially grown-up play, and even an apparently passive audience joins in the game by suspending its disbelief and pretending not to see that the drama woven around it is deception.

There is no theatre without playfulness. Play is the lifeblood of rehearsal. It breathes life into the empty husk of the text. The most faithfully rendered production, the most slavishly accurate repetition, will not produce anything worth experiencing unless the audience feels engaged in 'play'. Even in the midst of dramatic scenes of violence, treachery and abuse, actors are playing together and co-operating. If they didn't, it would be impossible for them to communicate the scene. As the audience we allow ourselves to be seduced and emotionally manipulated. In return, we can have all the thrills of living dangerously without having to suffer the consequences. We collude with the actors by imaginatively supporting their fantasy and temporarily 'forgetting' that the moments they suffer are not real. We become players: we join in the game and access once more the playful part of ourselves we may have given up in order to become adults.

CHILD'S PLAY

Play is the daily occupation of infants. They weave and resolve dramatic situations from their imaginations using play. Their play is totally committed, all-consuming and deadly serious. At the same time they, and all of us who were once children, instinctively know how to bring their imaginations into the world. Simple characterization ('I'll be the pirate'), the apportionment of roles ('You can be my prisoner'), the situation and setting ('We're on the sea. That table's the island') and the use of special techniques ('Teddy says he hates you') are employed with an ease that many directors and actors would envy, since the language of images and symbols is the natural language of children. The point about child's play is that it is *purposeful*. Children are essentially in rehearsal. In play they create and test rules, explore relationships and dare to live out antisocial thoughts and dangerous feelings. Even if it all ends in tears, no matter. Children are using play to rehearse encounters with their audience, which is the world. They are the models for game-playing actors and directors, who would do well to note their spontaneity, invention, simplicity and imagery, but above all their purposefulness.

GAMES

Games as Play

The game is a directed form of structured play. Someone who suggests the game and proposes the rules usually leads it. Agreement to the game and rules is like a contract between the players: it is a miniature social contract and creates in the company a sense of safety in play. The rules can be altered by common agreement as the game develops. Everyone knows what games are, since we all played them as children. They can quickly create a sense of community in companies whose members are from highly diverse backgrounds. Games can trigger strong memories of significant, sometimes life-shaping events. On one hand they have connotations of pleasure and joy and can generate lightness and childlike energy among the players; they also have their dark side, since the playground is a cruel world in which exclusion and rejection also feature. A skilful game player can take a company into all of these areas, and the great advantage of the game as a rehearsal tool is that it can be adapted precisely to meet the director's rehearsal objectives.

When Games are Appropriate to Rehearsal

Since the game is a precise tool, it follows that it is best practised with clear rehearsal objectives in mind. These objectives vary according to the rehearsal phase, and where games may be appropriate they have been indicated in the following chapters. Games are a language, and the rehearsal room is desperate for languages other than thoughts and words, which explore text and create theatre. Actors are 'body and soul' artists who need to work physically and with their feelings as well as with their intellects. Moscow Arts rehearsals in which actors sat on their backsides for months – sometimes years – analysing texts without moving their bodies sound like actors' nightmares. At the end of the process your brain knows everything but your body still knows nothing. Games allow actors to work physically and interactively, and are useful to rehearsal so long as they are not simply used as 'time wasters' by directors who don't know what to do next, or who wish to appear vaguely experimental.

Parallel Worlds

When working with text, games are best used in parallel with the scene being worked on. They are good for creating equivalent atmospheres,

tempi or movement styles, and it is often useful to construct a game to be played from time to time during the rehearsal as a visceral reminder to the actor of the physical dynamics of the scene.

There are, of course, no hard and fast rules for the use of games, but here are some general categories of sessions. Examples of game sequences are given at the end of the chapter.

Icebreakers

Why do directors invariably start rehearsals with a readthrough and an introduction to the play? Probably because the director is as nervous as the actors, and needs a totally prepared plan of action for the first meeting! Readthrough and introduction convey a massive amount of information to the actor, and if this is done on first rehearsal actors are in no position to take it in. They are too busy being pleasant to each other, making sure they do or say nothing that might make them look silly, weighing up the director and other actors, wondering if they're going to get paid. Under these circumstances an interactive, introductory session might be appropriate. Actors can talk to and touch each other in a game session without being responsible for what they say or do, since someone else, usually the director, will run it. When the verbal and physical ice has been broken and the session has achieved one or two simple tasks, set through games, players may have gained the confidence to relax, contribute to the rehearsal process, listen and even hear what others say.

Gaspers

These are single games prepared by the director, for use when the rehearsal process sinks into 'conference' stage, involving a lot of analysis and discussion. It's important to deal with the issue under discussion, but protracted argument quickly becomes time-consuming and counterproductive. It's often a more efficient use of time to work quickly, physically and interactively through a game before returning to the issue. The game allows the company to experience each other afresh and come at the issue in such a way that less articulate members can contribute. The leader can make the theme of the game relevant to the matter under discussion (*see* The 'Key Signature' Variables of Games, page 59).

Warm Ups
Warm up is the best way to use games when rehearsing a text. A brief sequence of games at the start of a rehearsal will not only establish a physical, contacting and interactive company culture, but may explore themes, atmospheres and relationships relevant to the rehearsal that follows. In this way the company gets a physical, pre-verbal sense of the task in hand. Directors can warm actors into specific scenes or moments within scenes if the director has clearly defined the issue to be explored in the game. The issue might be a playful moment in a couple relationship, for example. The director devises a light competitive physical game with an easy goal (*see* page 65), the pair play the game, then the text, and then they deliver the text while playing the game and so on. The object is to get the playful essence of the game into the specific moment in the scene.

Theatre Making
Games are the backbone of a devising rehearsal. The vast array of storytelling and acting-out games are useful triggers for creating material. Because the game is active and physical, it is more sympathetic to the actor than writing, which is a highly non-actor activity. Game and devising are dealt with in more detail in Chapter 8.

Creative Game Method
Most theatre practitioners have a bank of games to draw on, gleaned from long experience of their own and others' workshops. It's useful to

---

Exercise – Developing a Vocabulary of Games

1. Write out a list of the titles of ten games you enjoyed playing as a child.
2. Select one of the games and describe it in its simplest form, using no more than three rules.
3. Repeat this for all of the games on your list; this will be your 'reference list'.

---

collect games – indeed actors and directors would do well to keep a notebook of any ideas that work. However, it is a simple matter to invent your own rehearsal games, so here is a method for deconstructing children's games and rebuilding them in different forms, a single game producing many games, each tailored precisely to a particular purpose. This method was invented by Ed Berman in the 1960s and developed by his colleagues – myself included – for use in therapeutic, community and rehearsal settings. A complete account of the process would fill another book, but the following notes should get you going. I will assume you have a vocabulary of games. If not, acquire one immediately using the exercise above. Play out your ideas with actors at the first possible opportunity. Try out lots of ideas so that you don't get too attached to any of them. Above all, don't give up or feel you've failed if something doesn't work first time.

Freedom Within the Framework
The framework of a game is its structure, its nuts and bolts. The framework consists of all of the technical aspects of a game. Children often adopt or create games using very simple frameworks and few rules. If the game is popular it is played over and over again to the point of boredom until more rules, objectives and ways of

playing are bolted on, extending the framework. A game is like a fairy story that has an archetypal core, understood by all, plus culturally specific 'bolt-ons', which vary from community to community.

The game is an effective starting point for exploring rehearsal ideas through play: the 'big idea' explored at the start of the rehearsal, or the smaller ideas that explore issues arising from specific scenes. Games make good starting points because the framework of the game provides a clear boundary to playing. The game is a safe playing space and all the players know the rules before it starts. If the leader knows how to sequence a game, it can be made more difficult or challenging step by step, exploiting the confidence of the players as their confidence grows.

The players feel free to play because of the framework of the game. Games contain just enough information to facilitate action and the apparent restraints of the rules of the game make it safer to play. Instructions that appear to be totally permissive like 'Play around for a bit' or 'Do something' or 'Entertain me' are famously impossible to respond to – players would have to invent the framework for play. The skill of constructing a game is to create a framework that facilitates action around the rehearsal task.

GAMES – CUSTOMIZING TECHNIQUES

Goal and Function in Games

This is an important and very useful aspect of game analysis. The 'goal' of a game is its objective. In a competitive game, it is to win. 'Functions' of a game, however, are what you have to do in order to achieve your goal.

In a game of football or hockey, for example, you try to score more goals or points than your opponent does. This is the goal of the game. To do this you have to work together, exercise vigorously, accept your role in the team, practise skills, engage in physical contact, exercise control, play to the rules, and so on. These are the functions of the game.

While the game is being played the players are focused totally on the goal. Because their attention is elsewhere, players engage thoroughly with functions such as teamwork and physical contact in a subconscious way. Once experienced, these functions can be explored deliberately.

When considering the 'point' of a game, the leader should consider all of its functions, because that is where the rehearsal value of a game lies. Players can be induced to explore delicate areas in games, if their attention is focused upon its goal.

Goal	Functions
(How you win)	*(What you must do to succeed)*
To score most points/goals	Be physically fit
	Know and play out your role in the team
	Develop specific physical skills
	Be physically coordinated
	Communicate effectively with your *teammates*
	Know and observe the rules
	Know and observe the etiquette of the game

Exercise

This exercise uses the game 'Grandmother's footsteps', where one person turns their back and the others go to the other end of the room. They creep up on the person whose back is turned, but if that person turns and sees any movement, the person moving must go back and start again. The goal of the game is to touch the person whose back is turned.

1. List all the functions of the game.
2. Imagine a play whose world might be approached by rehearsing those functions.
3. Imagine a rehearsal or a rehearsal stage for which this game might be a good warm up.
4. Repeat the exercise using a different game on your list.

Grandmother's footsteps. Goal: to touch grandmother. Functions: physical concentration, movement with control and focus of attention.

The 'Framework' Variables of Games

There are a number of elements to the framework of a game and each one of them can be altered. This gives us great control over the playing of games and can produce many games from one. By gradually adjusting a game, the session leader can edge the players step by step towards a given rehearsal objective. It is quite possible to play for two hours using only one game and its variations.

The Line-Up of Players

Line-up means how the players are grouped. Here are some line-ups:

- **Teams** Players are divided into two teams, as in a football game.
- **Pairs** Playing with a partner.
- **Chaos** The players play at random with whoever they encounter.
- **Clumps** A number of small groups.
- **Whole group** Everyone co-operating.
- **Circle** Everyone can see everyone else at all times.
- **One against the group** Usually the individual has a role and the group has a role.

Number of Players

How many players are playing at any given time? Sometimes, everyone plays; at other times, pairs or small groups may take turns to 'perform' to the other players, who watch. The game may evolve from all playing to one performing to the rest, or the reverse.

The Rules of the Game

The maturity of a game can often be deduced from its burden of rules. The core of a game can usually be expressed in two or three rules. Rules can be added, subtracted or substituted, to fit your purpose.

The Field of Play

This is the playing area. Usually the whole room, but you might like to play through the whole building or spill the game into the street. On the other hand you may want to constrain the field by dividing the room with chairs and designating a playing area. Many high-energy games have an optimum field of play and have to be adapted to larger or smaller spaces.

Time Limits

The session leader might set a time limit. If brief – a minute or two – this will produce a burst of activity, since players compete instinctively with the clock. Alternatively, the game can be played at length until it decays naturally. The session leader will sense the point at which a game is played out. In chaos or pairs, players will start to give up, and as the focus falls on the remaining players the pressure to stop will increase. The game can also be played until the goal has been achieved.

Referee

You can choose to have a referee or decide not to have one. You can use a panel of referees or you can all referee by voting.

The Goal

The goal is where the intention of the players is focused. The goal must be simple, easily understandable and achievable. The goal can be to win, or it may be a co-operative goal – perhaps the players make something.

Exercise

1. Use Grandmother's footsteps (*see* previous page). The standard line-up is 'one against the group'.
2. Consider playing this game with a different line-up. In pairs? Clumps? Two teams?
3. Invent another game by changing only the line-up of Grandmother's footsteps.

ABOVE: *Circle line-up.*
RIGHT: *Passing the buck.*

The 'Key Signature' Variables of Games

If the framework is the structure of a game, effectively its hardware, the key signature is its software or content. If the framework is the 'what' of playing, the key signature is the 'how'. The key signature can be varied in a number of categories, and this gives us further opportunities to create alternative versions of a single game:

Working in small groups.

- **Theme** 'As though' you were at a party, 'as though' you were all slightly drunk, 'as though' you were all five-year-olds, 'as though' one of you had betrayed the others, 'as though' you were all sexually attracted to each other, like the Wild West.
- **Characterization** Do it like chickens, like Restoration Fops, like beggars, transforming into animals, unable to speak.
- **Mood** Do it sadly, joyfully, loudly, sullenly, shyly, boastfully, beautifully, evasively, in an atmosphere of grief.
- **Tempo** In slow motion, complete the game in two (timed) minutes.

Variables of Competition and Co-operation

There are a number of playing possibilities on the spectrum of choices between co-operation and competition in games. Games can be both co-operative and competitive. In football, teams must work co-operatively in order to win. There are invariably co-operative elements even in the apparently most competitive games. Broadly speaking, if the goal of the game is easily achievable by an individual, co-

---

Exercises

- Select a game from your reference list and give it a key signature of your own invention, in any of the categories listed (*see* left).
- Imagine you are creating a brief warm-up session for *Romeo and Juliet*. Select a theme from the play, create a key signature from some aspect of the theme and apply it to two or three games from your reference list.
- Alter the games using any of the variables (*see* left) to make them suitable for your imaginary rehearsal.

---

operation is unlikely. Setting the goal will fundamentally affect the relationship between the players.

Competitive games are usually highly energized and generate motivation. Competitive games can be repeated in a co-operative form, so that the energy generated in the first playing can be turned towards constructive, even creative, co-operative play. These possibilities offer another range of choices to game players:

- **Individually competitive** Somebody wins. Possibly others are knocked out and become observers.
- **Groups/teams compete** A group/team wins. This can easily be created in co-operative form where teams 'make and show'.
- **Individuals/teams compete against the clock** Timed exercises.
- **Players meet the leader's challenge**.

GAMES – PLAYING TECHNIQUES

Limited Objectives
The cardinal rule in game-playing is 'start simple and build'. A collection of individuals begins to feel like a group or a company by working towards agreed common goals and by achieving common objectives. Games can assist the process of consolidating the company in common experience and objectives. This identity can be built through the achievement of small objectives in games.

Exercise

- Use 'tag', a competitive game with a one-against-the-group line-up. The person who is 'it' transfers the 'it' by touching another person. The group avoids the person who is 'it'. If you remove the 'avoidance' rule so the players no longer avoid the person who is 'it', we now have a co-operative game.
- Invent something for the person to do while they are 'it', for example they could act like an animal, tell a story or sing!
- Using a competitive game from your reference list, remove the competition.
- Add a rule so that the players can make or build something in the game.
- *See* 'devising' (Chapter 8) for developments of this idea.

Setting up a 'team's' line-up.

Focus of Attention in Games

Game leaders in rehearsal can control the pressure on the players by controlling the focus of attention. How likely is it that others will notice if you make a mistake? If it is likely we say the focus is high. If it is unlikely we say the focus is low or shattered. There are risks attached to adult play. Most of us fear failure or humiliation, especially with people we don't know very well, so focus of attention is important in game play, especially at the start of a session. High focus has high performance pressure, low focus allows for exploration and process work. It is highly facilitating. The number of players affects the focus. If everyone is playing, the noise level and the activity is high. The focus of attention is low and the game is easier to play than if only two are playing, watched by the others. It follows that you can rehearse games by playing simultaneously – in pairs or chaos – then focusing attention by playing a pair, an individual or a small group at a time, watched by the other players. Different line-ups focus attention differently. The circle is usually high-focus and chaos usually low.

Methods of shattering focus include raising the level of activity or the noise level; or playing in the dark, or with eyes closed, or lying on the floor looking at the ceiling (no/low eye contact).

Leadership

Though games and games sessions rely on a leader, leadership can easily be handed over, or handed around the players in the company. This gives a richer sense of ownership among players and gives the director the chance to

Whole group clump.

step out of the play altogether and plan the next task. Games that have a one-against-the-group line-up, or that sequence leaders by handing over leadership through a cueing mechanism ('tag', for example), give the session leader the chance to demonstrate a game as leader and then pass on the leadership. This will subsequently pass through the group without further invention while the leader observes the play.

How to Lead a Game or Game Session

In order to become an expert game leader you have to do it a lot. Books are no substitute for jumping in at the deep end! The worst that can happen is that you get a general rather than a particular result. At the very least, games are good 'ensemble' practice, so however inexperienced you are, the time is never totally wasted.

Here is a checklist for session leading.

- Smile, look relaxed, be light! It lowers the stakes for the players and makes them more adventurous.
- If it is your first session with a company who don't know each other, remember that they are at least as nervous as you are.
- Start with something simple and easy to achieve.
- Use the simplest version of the game and set it up with two or three rules at the most.
- What you do communicates more information and is more powerful than what you say, so demonstrate the rules as you set them up.
- Always cue the start of a game. Participation usually fails because the players don't know when to start and fear humiliation. 'When I say go!' will do.
- Build up a complex game step by step. Always start simple and play the game through each time you add a complication. Doing is always better than talking.

- Unless it is absolutely not your directing style, join in. Of course directors have to watch, but there will be times when you can play and it gives you and the company a wholly different sense of each other.
- If you play in pairs and you have an odd number, partner the player who is left over after the pairing up.
- Never say 'lets play a game': it sounds desperate! Just get on with it.
- Get into the habit of saying 'well done'. It doesn't hurt and is good for morale. There will be plenty of other occasions for ruthless honesty.
- Plan a couple of games but never the whole session. You should be working to a broad plan but responding to the group in the present moment.

Planning Games into the Rehearsal Process

- Use games as warm-ups before all early rehearsals, especially where the cast don't know each other. Games should be active, physical, interactive and fun.
- Use games as part of the physical warm-up that should precede all company rehearsals.
- During the analysis phase of a text rehearsal, explore the culture and the atmosphere of the world of the play by using games that give a similar feel. Use games as analogies, to give the actors a visceral sensation of your ideas.
- Once lines have been learned and the scene 'set', use games to lend texture to the scene. Have the actors play the scene while also playing an appropriate game. The game must be buried in the scene. An onlooker must not be able to see that a game is being played at all until one player wins.
- Late in rehearsal, play the games you used during analysis in order to revisit the vividness of your early discoveries.
- Also use games for devising rehearsals (*see* Chapter 8).

Example of Game Sequencing

This is the start of an 'icebreaking' session to introduce a group of strangers working together for the first time

Leader's Instructions	Function of the Game	Game Theory
'Sit on chairs in a circle'	Circle is part of the 'starting ritual'	
'Two claps, followed by two spaces' (leader, then group, does this)	Limited initial participation	Set limited objective
'Same game but in the space, starting with me and going round to my left, make a sound which shows how you are feeling now' (do it)	Increase commitment by achieving a series of limited objectives	Demonstrate, then get them to do it Key signature = feelings
'Same game, add a gesture to the sound you make'	Extend to physical and vocal commitment	
'Two claps and two spaces. In the space touch the person to your left. Two claps and in the space touch the person to your right' (leader demonstrates, group plays)	Physical contact between players	Adding a rule The limited time and quick rhythm prevent self-consciousness
'Same game again, but this time you mustn't touch in the same place twice. *Go!*'	All over contact Slapstick and laughter	Add a rule Cue the start immediately with '*Go!*' to cut out thinking time
'Think of someone you want to sit next to, who you're not next to at the moment. Choose someone for no reason at all. Keep that person in your mind. We're going to play the last game again, but when I say "Now!" go and sit next to the person in your mind. *Go!*' (The last game is played again. When the leader says 'Now!' The circle breaks into chaos. Some achieve the aim. The circle reforms.)	High energy Break up cliques who usually sit together Physical and verbal contact	Add a rule Individuals compete to fulfil the game – energy rises Contact and reforming the circle are functions of the game
'You have two minutes to find out one thing you didn't know before, from as many people in the room as you can manage. *Go!*'	Verbal contact with maximum number of contacts Continue to break up 'safe' sub-groups in the players Permission to assert and 'butt-in'	

Leader's Instructions	Function of the Game	Game Theory
'Put your hand on the person nearest to you but not someone who is touching you. When I say "Go!" rub that person with your hand. Go! Rub as many people in the room as you can manage ... use your shoulders ... use your backsides'	Breaking physical barriers Limited objective Non-verbal communication	Maintain the energy through time limit Change field from circle to chaos – facilitate chance encounters Change the key signature of the last game from verbal to physical

Example of Late Rehearsal Warm-up for a Production of a Restoration Comedy

The object is to sensitize the company to movement, use of space and focus of attention in the restoration manner

Description of Core Game	Activity
Finger sword fighting Functions: Play, exercise, focus concentration, compete, contact play in pairs.	Each partner places one hand on the small of their back, palm out and extends the finger of their other hand (this is their 'sword') They must touch the palm of their partner with the tip of their sword finger, without letting their palm be touched. Three 'kills' and you're dead!
First variation Function: 360 degree awareness of space	Change the line-up to chaos Anyone may kill anyone in the room Last alive wins
Second variation Function: A sense of style in space	Add a key signature, 'poise' Let the back of the hand support the small of the back, maintaining posture throughout If the hand is stabbed, posture collapses Add a rule: players who forget poise are 'socially dead' at the discretion of the leader, who referees
Third variation Functions: to play the text honestly, using the game as a point of total concentration	Tie a thick ribbon round the waist of each player, tied with a bow at the back Play in heeled shoes if possible The player's hands are now free to unlace the bow Play small altercations and love scenes in this way, using the text, but ignoring blocking and staging Players must play the scene while preparing to unlace their partners if the chance arises Scenes become highly charged, sexy, and show skilful use of space if the game is thoroughly 'buried' in the scene

7   USING IMPROVISATION

WHY IMPROVISE?

Improvisation is the basic tool of the 'theatre-making actor', and can also be powerful in the exploration of text. However, it is only one of many tools and, among all the rehearsal skills, improvisation seems most prone to the vagaries of fad and fashion. It can appear to be the badge of creativity. Some directors will almost apologize for not using it, and others use it unnecessarily without completely knowing why. There is nothing inherently inventive or even creative about improvisation, and impros allowed to drift endlessly on by a director not sure what to do next can actually kill creative energy in the company. The rule of thumb when rehearsing texts is to regard impro as a tool that can help solve problems. 'If it isn't broken, don't fix it': if you are devising through impro, work to clear objectives or you'll waste time.

Like games, improvisation gets spontaneous play into the rehearsal room. Unlike games, energy is not sustained by a competitive or co-operative dynamic, or by the creation of a 'goal'. Improvisation invariably develops its own rhythm and style, triggered, for example, by a given circumstance, character choice, setting, prop, word, phrase or gesture, from which the actor makes a specific exploration. Usually there is no end point – you have to stop it. Thus improvisation is a working space set up by the director for use by the actor. The director invents a trigger, and sometimes suggests a framework of changeable rules, circumstances or intentions, which focus the playing towards the rehearsal objective.

STAGE 1
PLANNING AN IMPRO REHEARSAL

Be rigorous in defining your objectives for the rehearsal. Improvisation for its own sake is hard work, unsatisfying and ultimately demoralizing. A good session will yield results on a number of levels, so one objective doesn't necessarily exclude others. Actors always benefit from playing together: physical play breaks down inhibitions, verbal improvisation is a good warm-up for scripted dialogue, and spontaneous play helps remind the actor that theatre always takes place in the immediate present. These are general objectives – they will happen more or less whatever you do. Beyond this, you can seek specific outcomes for your rehearsal process and achieve these at the same time.

When planning the impro rehearsal, take the stage of rehearsal into account. Objectives in the early stages of rehearsal, apart from 'icebreaking', include information gathering, exploring character choices, exploring the implications of style (for example, is the play realistic, expressionist, classical?), creating material, and 'experiencing' the world of the play.

During the middle stage of rehearsal, impro offers opportunities such as interacting characters to develop relationships, exploring narrative through interactive play, playing scenes on and off the text and improvising within the rules of the chosen style.

Late rehearsals offer objectives such as using different points of concentration to create 'texture' (*see* Chapter 9), playing 'events' in character and exploring alternative or opposite choices.

STAGE 2
SETTING OBJECTIVES FOR YOURSELF AND THE ACTORS

Plan your session, but not in laborious detail. You don't want to read your instructions from a piece of paper, which would look very unspontaneous! Keep two elements clear in your mind: the trigger or starting point of rehearsal, and the outcome or learning process relevant to the rehearsal stage and the production.

STAGE 3
SETTING UP THE IMPRO

Before beginning the session, set out the playing area and decide how the observers will relate to the players. Some actors will be improvising while others watch and eventually comment and take their turn in the playing space. The relationship between them is important. You might choose to use the whole space with the 'audience' sitting round the wall, or have the audience sitting in a line in front of a small, tight playing area. It depends on the playing atmosphere you want to create. Consider some of the options outlined in the previous chapter on games.

Remind the company of the theme and objective of the session: it is your responsibility to hold the company to the objective and develop the theme through the session. Improvisation is essentially research for you and the company, so always set a point of concentration for each impro. This might be an aspect of characterization, style or narrative.

Briefly set out the rules of play. For example you might say:

I'll set up the impro, and you play in and see what happens. If you do something unexpected,

that's good – we might stumble on something new. We'll watch. If it doesn't work it'll be because I haven't set it up right and I'll try again. Whatever happens, keep going unless I stop you.

In this way you include the whole company, players and observers in the process, and you reassure the actors that you will leave them free to play without fear of being made to look stupid if they misunderstand your instructions. It may sound like a lot of speeches: in fact, you must be brief and get to action as quickly as possible. The longer you speak the more passive the actors will become, and it is essential that they feel they are responsible and working for themselves, rather than trying to please you. You must seek verbal or physical contributions from them as quickly as possible.

STAGE 4
PLAYING WITH ACTORS

Actors can't help trying to entertain each other and this can kill the session, since mutual entertainment isn't its object. Jokey, 'funny' sessions, overappreciated by the observing actors, will be accompanied by rising competitiveness, which will eventually destroy the rehearsal. Actors want to please, and fear failure or humiliation. It follows that early impros should be very simple and a bit boring. This lowers the stakes and sets a tone of easy acceptance. All actors know that you never get any better by trying harder. As they realize that your expectations are below their failure threshold, they unwind, watch, listen and respond, and their natural creativity can show itself. The following guidelines might help:

- Let the early impros 'go on a bit' – don't fall into the trap of trying to entertain the actors.
- Discourage all judgemental responses – good or bad – from the observing actors.

They have to go on next, and will only wind each other up!
- Every time you stop an impro say 'good!'.
- When discussing the impro make it clear that you have no interest in whether anyone enjoyed it. Focus instead on remembering what actually happened and what we should do next.

STAGE 5
SOME IMPRO OPTIONS

Focus 'Game' Impros
A simple and effective use of impro is to impose simple rules upon the playing of a scene. You can improvise a scene that develops the relationship between two characters, or that exposes some aspect of a given character, then develop the impro in the following ways:

Play the Scene in Gibberish
Gibberish is a made-up language, not a foreign language. The point of concentration is to really be speaking to each other, so you could go into plain language at any time. The use of this exercise is that it frees up the body, forces the actor to become physically expressive while relieving him or her from searching for the right word.

Play without Words
Brecht suggests that the actors rehearse by pretending that they are playing the scene behind a thick sheet of glass, so that the audience can't hear the words. This is also good for encouraging full physical expression.

Play in Double Time
The point of concentration is not to flatten out the scene. All of the pauses, the shape of the dialogue, the expression and the tempo must all remain, except that the scene is played at twice the normal speed. It's good for weeding out actors' flabby 'thinking' time, encouraging decisiveness and flow in the playing of the

Impro warm-up – a group statue.

scene. Remind the actor to avoid tensing up, by playing down the many mistakes that will occur. Repeat until the actors are confident and accurate. Use these three exercises for story-telling impros (*see* Plan 1, page 72).

Shadowing
Shadowing means that each actor has an assistant. The possibilities are endless:

- The actor speaks, the shadow gives the stage directions.
- The shadow prompts all the lines, the actor invents actions.
- The actor speaks, the shadow speaks the subtext, for example, 'That's what he says, but this is what he really thinks.'

No Circumstance Impro
It is possible to improvise and develop scenes without preparing physical circumstances or

making character choices. Character and circumstance arise from the spontaneous actions and dialogue of the improvisers, sometimes just from dumb show and gesture. Examples are given in Chapter 12.

A no-circumstance impro session is usually run by the director as a series of exercises. The exercise is then analysed, adapted and repeated, according to the objective of the session. This sort of session is playful, energized and immediate. It is useful for getting actors out of their heads and into their wits. It can be used at all stages of rehearsal, initially to develop professional trust, immediacy and creative challenge among the company members. Late in rehearsal it is useful to develop or re-create immediacy when repetition may have drained the life from a production.

Limited Circumstance

Here, some circumstances from the play being rehearsed are put into the impro, using broad brush strokes. In the following example, limited circumstances use character and relationship without setting.

Triggering a 'no circumstance' impro using a gesture and eye contact. Only use speech if necessary.

The Set-Up
Four actors sit in a circle, around a single actor in the centre. In this example of a devised play, each actor has a well developed character, they know their relationship to the other characters and the rehearsal process is well advanced:

Character X = a middle-aged man in the circle
Character 1 = his worried wife, who interprets his strange behaviour as concealing a fatal illness
Character 2 = his pregnant mistress, who hysterically pleads with him to leave his wife
Character 3 = his financial advisor, patiently trying to sell him a pension
Character 4 = his camp son, who challenges him to 'loosen up' and have a few drinks

How It Works
1. Each character in turn improvises for a few minutes with character X, developing the thread of a scene. X then goes into the circle.
2. Each character, in turn and on the director's cue, resumes their scene with X, who must adapt to the new situation without stopping or breaking the flow.
3. The pressure is carefully increased by speeding up the cueing or by getting X to play with two or more characters at once.
4. X begins to experience the pressure of his circumstances, and this experience is fragmented and discontinuous, rather than reasonable and logical, as it would be if he were working to a psychological interpretation.

This exercise works well in rehearsals of plays where the pressure on a single lead character is intense.

Example: Hedda Gabler *by Ibsen*
X = Hedda Gabler
Character 1 = Tesman, her husband
Character 2 = Lovborg, the man from her past
Character 3 = Judge Brack

*Warming up for an 'event'
impro at the stock
exchange.*

Example: Woyzek *by Buchner*
X = Woyzek
Character 1 = the Sergeant, goading Woyzek to fight him
Character 2 = Marie, who cradles Woyzek and sings him a lullaby
Character 3 = the knife seller who patiently describes the cutting qualities of each of his knives
Character 4 = the Captain who procures a shave by giving Woyzek orders

Improvisation Using Given Circumstances

These improvisations are carefully prepared, re-creating a specific location perhaps with furniture, and marking doors for entrances. 'Circumstances' may include location, immediate factors, characterization, actions and activities. The actors do not step onto the stage without answering the questions 'Where am I?', 'When is it?', 'What do I want?', 'How can I get it?' and 'Who am I?' (*see* Chapter 14). Given circumstance exercises are therefore very specific, though the actors need considerable skill to work these exercises spontaneous-

ly, since they have to remember a lot of circumstantial detail and are therefore inclined to try to think their way through the impro and become physically tense.

Actors may use these exercises to explore relationships, aspects of their character, moments important to the actor's understanding of the role, though not written into the play. *See* Chapter 12 for examples.

Simultaneous Playing

Director-Led 1: Guided Dream
A whole-company imaginative warm-up led by the director. The actors work alone in their space.

1. The director, by giving a series of image-oriented instructions, encourages the actor to imaginatively 'see' the character they are playing.
2. The director then allows the actor to take control of the imagined character by engaging with it in simple play.
3. The actor then allows the imagined character to 'possess' him or her. Michael Checkov

suggests that the actor 'lend' the character his or her body.

4. The characters play together.
5. The director talks the actors back into their own bodies and out of the exercise.

The director should work from notes to preserve, repeat or rehearse useful events produced in the impro. The actors will be pleased to recreate and refine your noted moments if you ask. With a little help, they will always be able to remember, or they aren't really actors. Encourage the actors to note down their discoveries.

This may sound a bit esoteric. In fact it is very practical and often very useful as research. An example of an advanced guided dream is given in Plan 2 on page 73. The example happens to be for a Jacobean play, but you can use this exercise for any play.

Director-Led 2: Simultaneous Exploration
The director asks the actors to come to rehearsal having each decided on a simple activity appropriate to their character. Activities like dressing to go out, writing a letter or doing some work appropriate to the character would be suitable. Actors might be asked to incorporate a prop or object precious to the character into the activity. Actors establish a small territory in the rehearsal space, and work alone on their activity. The director moves round the room, discussing actor's choices and their implications for the production. Occasionally the director will halt the proceedings and everyone will watch one person work. This is useful during early- to mid-rehearsal, since it gives real exploratory opportunity to the actor, while allowing the director to observe the company at work and concentrate on issues of style and consistency.

'Event' Impros
Two events are outlined in Plan 3 on page 74. Events give actors the chance to 'live' their role. This is sometimes useful for detailed realistic

work. The object is to sustain character in all circumstances over a significant period of time, as far as possible in the actual circumstances. This helps establish the distance between the personality of the actor and the character.

STAGE 6
FEEDBACK AND RERUNS

Feedbacks and reruns allow you to focus and refine your work. Obviously you can discuss and rerun an exercise, but you should feel free to stop a simultaneous impro at any time or work on moments from a guided dream once the sequence is over.

Triggering the impro by physicalizing the relationship.

STAGE 7
INTEGRATING THE IMPRO INTO THE REHEARSAL PROCESS

The director's role throughout is to highlight and retain what in the improvisation is most useful to the production. While observing and developing an exercise with actors, get into the habit of saying 'good' as a way of halting the impro. Tell the actor what is most useful in the impro and indicate what is less relevant, or superfluous. Encourage others to talk in this way rather than in terms of good and bad, which are not at all useful to the process and can set up obstacles to play. The actor is researching and exploring, not performing. When you return to the production you should have some concrete references that you can use to explain what you want from the actor. Actors are very good at recalling what they have *done*, as opposed to what they *said*, since physical memory is at the root of the actor's craft.

Plan 1

Play: *Arabian Nights*, dir. John Perry, 1997

The version by Mike Alfreds with Shared Experience, a storytelling play intercutting narrative and scene play with a highly physical style and personal contact between the cast and audience throughout.

Rehearsal Stage

This impro was planned for an early rehearsal; at the point of the second read-through, stopping for detailed notes on style, discussing the playing options within the 'world' of the play. This was one of the impro sessions, interspersed with discussion and readings to give the cast a variety of experiences of the text.

Impro Task

To explore the style of the play from the point of view of the audience/actor relationship.

Objectives

1. To explore the actor/audience relationship in narrative theatre.
2. To understand and rehearse the skill of narrating and scene playing, and moving from one to the other.

Description of Session (1½ Hours)

1. In turn, one member of the company told the others a one-minute fairy story.
2. We discussed the natural inclination of the storyteller to treat the audience like children. We explored ways to storytell adult-to-adult.
3. We story-told in pairs, using a 'supportive pair' in which individuals finish each other's sentences and a 'critical pair' in which individuals contradicted or amended their partner's account.
4. We explored the 'tone of voice' in storytelling – absolute scripted certainty versus the tentativeness of real memory recall.
5. We explored narrating options, using a narrator and 'acting out' actors.
6. We put the narrator in the audience, stage left and stage right, above and below the actors, and discussed the different effects.
7. We let each character narrate and speak in the scene.
8. We explored the technical issue of the 'extended aside' as the actor moved in and out of the scene to narrate directly to the audience.

Play: *'Tis Pity She's a Whore* by John Ford, dir. John Perry, 1996

A late Jacobean play, in a cut-down version, set in the seventeenth-century world of James I and the conventions of bloody revenge tragedy.

Rehearsal Stage

A mid-stage rehearsal, when scenes are being rehearsed individually; the company is somewhat fragmented and rarely together. A full company improvisation session is an opportunity for individuals to see and participate in each other's work, and for the director to consider how to bind the scenes and the actors into a single, unified world.

Impro Tasks

- To explore, in a physical and sensory way, specific character choices.
- To give the company a common experience of character transformation.

Outcomes

The actor literally gets a 'sense' of the character, working not from the logical thinking, but from the senses, which are not always consistent, but bring the character to life.

Instructions from the Director to the Actors

1. 'Stand in a neutral position, shoulders relaxed, back of the head as though held by a puppet string from the ceiling, base of the spine released so that the spine is straight and extended without tension. Knees slightly flexed, hands open. Concentrate on exhaling, let the in breath take care of itself ...'
2. 'Close your eyes. Imagine your see your character in a picture ... See the whole picture ... are you seeing an oil painting or a line drawing, a photograph? Is it light or dark? Does the picture give you a particular feeling? A happy or sad atmosphere? Is it an inside or outside scene? What room or what landscape? With other people or alone? Is it day or night? What time of day? Identify all the objects in the picture apart from your character ...' and so on.
3. 'Let your character in the picture become a silhouette. Note the outline of your character. Now imagine that the picture dissolves, just leaving the silhouette standing. Let it walk towards you. As it approaches be aware of the size of the character. Smaller or larger than you? Heavier or lighter? Thinner or fatter? See the colour tones of the clothes, the cut of the cloth – clean or dirty. Smell the character. Is the face coarser or finer than yours, lighter or darker?' ... and so on. You can invent simple manipulation exercises here: 'Get the character to walk up and down, turn round.'
4. 'Let the character walk behind you and slip their hands and arms into your hands and arms. Let your arms and hands transform into their arms and hands. Let them 'possess' your hands. How do your hands change? Coarser or finer? What do these new hands do? Heavier or lighter arms? Do the same with the legs and hips, with the trunk (does the heartbeat change? the nervous system? the beats and rhythms of the body?) and finally with the head (compare the eyes, the nose, hair, the mouth – are there any teeth in it?).'
5. 'When completely transformed, let the character explore the world using your body. Keep the actions simple.'

Meetings are possible between characters, but don't get too complicated and only do this with experienced groups.

At the end of the exercise, talk the actor back into their body by reversing the transformation process, first the head, then trunk, legs and finally hands. Give a minute to 'come back'.

Take notes during the exercise and afterwards talk about it. Inexperienced actors enjoy the transformation and become conscious of the details of the differences between them and their character, and therefore the transformation required.

Event Impros

Plays in which the characters create a chorus of feeling or which happen within a very distinct atmosphere, for example:

The world of the destitute (Gorky's *Lower Depths*, Euripedes' *Trojan Women*) or the world of the wealthy 'flapper' (plays by Wilde or Coward).

Rehearsal Stage

Late. Character and text should be in place. The object is to choose an appropriate real setting in which you can live your character and interact, in character, with ordinary people for, perhaps, half a day. You have to maintain the tempo of the character in the atmosphere of the world you create around you.

Impro Tasks

- To live out your character in the real world.
- To genuinely experience 'being' the character.
- To test the authenticity of your choices.
- To maintain the style and atmosphere back in the rehearsal room.

Outcome

- Awareness of the specific detail of speech, tempo and mannerism.
- Enhanced confidence and assurance.
- A sharpened sense of what does and doesn't work creates a clear analysis of character work.
- This is essentially a methodological approach to acting, authentic in the sense that it connects you as a person to your role and to the real world.

Description (Half or Whole Day)

The impro is in three stages:

1. *Plan* Brainstorm where you might go. Invent appropriate rules.
2. *Action* Improvise your scenario in the real world, maintaining character whatever happens.
3. *Feedback* Relate your experiences and witness each others.

Plan and Action

The destitute. You are going to spend a full day on the street with no money and no food, for example, under Waterloo Bridge. Rules: you only eat what you can beg or steal? Just enough clothes to keep you slightly uncomfortable? Spend the whole day alone? Or whatever rules you feel will help the authenticity. Remember you are playing! Try to discover the tempo or rhythm of a day on the streets.

The flapper. You are going to spend half a day 'flapping'. Dress up in your (or someone else's) most expensive clothes. Go to the most expensive shops in town and try everything on. Shoes, clothes, accessories. For example, if in London, shop in Mayfair, have tea at the Ritz. Buy absolutely nothing. Rules: dress each other, find everything funny, make jokes and laugh throughout, or only discuss golf, hilariously. Gossip loudly. Be a nuisance, make a fuss, don't notice. Arrange a 'feedback' party with alcohol in the evening. Feedback in character. Or whatever rules you like.

Feedback

The actors feedback to the company individually or in pairs or small groups, depending on the size of the company. Encourage them to feedback using the language of theatre, not the language of the lecture hall. The flappers could feedback in character at a party because that would be 'in character' for them. For more formal feedback, you could ask each actor or group to bring back three moments of theatre from their experience: these might be small scenes, atmospheric moments, or the creation of a character encountered as a real person on the streets.

8   THE DEVISING PROCESS

Devising means making your own theatre, rather than interpreting someone else's text. It includes building a text through rehearsal, adapting personal material, and transposing poems, prose extracts, traditional stories or visual material into a text or scenario. It includes any rehearsal process that starts with a partial or non-existent script. First drafts and workshop productions also require devising skills. Devising is a huge subject embracing a wide range of rehearsal situations, and this chapter will confine itself to general principles for planning and running devising rehearsals.

Devising is an increasingly important source of work for directors and actors, not only in the community/education/small touring part of the market, but also in every part of the subsidized sector. Established companies who play nothing but classical texts also need to create workshops as part of their touring and funding contracts.

THE DIRECTOR'S ROLE

Not all directors like devising. If you need to be in control from start to finish you might not be very good at it. You need flexibility, the ability to turn uncertainty to creative advantage, and to put up with the insecurity of actors who have no lines to learn. If you have a rigid view of the final show early in the rehearsal process you will find it difficult to draw out the full range of skills and talent in the actors and create a sense of ownership in the company. Devising is a collaborative art, which needs actors, designers and technicians to work together on equal terms. The director's ability to maintain morale is important if the creative energy of the company is not to be used up on bad group dynamics.

Because confidence and sense of progress are essential to the devising actor, directors must facilitate and encourage much more than if they were rehearsing a text. For most of the rehearsal period the director is in the same situation as the actor, collaborating to make a piece of theatre without being entirely sure of what will happen next. If, as the director, you wish to stand aside and critically evaluate the work, you must choose your moment with sensitivity and care since a badly chosen word to performers who have little to hold on to can take the work backwards rather than forwards. If you can write as well as direct, you can create a text from workshops and then direct it, combining devising with conventional rehearsal. Not many directors are competent to a professional level in both areas. Usually directors collaborate with actors who are creating roles and learning lines while they are developing the scenario, so that at the end of rehearsal a piece of theatre has been simultaneously created and rehearsed.

The devising process needs partners who can turn their hand to a number of tasks. As a director it helps to have confidence with sound and lights, to have some writing skills and an understanding of associated performance skills such as puppetry, storytelling, carnival, clown and so on. You need actors with some music and

The Collaborating Director

- Works by inspiring confidence in actors and the production team.
- Creates and discards enormous amounts of material.
- Fosters a culture of collaboration: enjoys sharing ideas and does not need to take all of the initiatives.
- Can let others lead, including designers, stage managers and technicians.
- Is able to say when he/she doesn't know what to do next!
- Is a facilitator, encouraging actors to bring all of their experience and skill to rehearsal and regarding this as a rehearsal resource.
- Has an effective method of recording rehearsal sessions.
- Can effectively lead improvisation and groupwork, having a method for creating material from these.
- Is flexible, allowing ideas to evolve and not being afraid to change his or her mind, even if it involves starting again.
- Is able to take and give over control as appropriate, but remains the final decision-taker.
- Leads the company through the decision-making process.
- Takes responsibility for the final show.
- Actors work 'with' and not 'for' this director.

World of George Orwell (dir. Deborah Yhip, 2001). All research material assembled under titles on the rehearsal room wall.

movement in them. You don't have to be expert in all or any of these but the broader the performance base of the company, the easier it will be to make theatre rather than literature.

SOURCES OF MATERIAL

The first step in the devising process – its springboard – is to find somewhere to start. It should be material that you find irresistible. Technically it can be almost anything, not only literature: art, song, history, a short story, news, music, personal affects, biography, clothes, film, or fragments of all of these. When you rehearse text you research its context, but when you devise, finding the springboard for your imagination will be the start of your research.

USING YOURSELF

You might start with the personal experience of members of the company. It may be based on an issue like sex, drugs, rock 'n roll, or it may explore a life stage like adolescence or parenthood. It may deal with the inner lives of the actors – their personal dreams and fantasies. This sort of work is very immediate. It gives an overwhelming sense of now, especially if explored in a fresh way by a young company. It works well if the audience and the actors hold the same social or political point of view, and want to publicly celebrate their views in the theatre.

There are two potential pitfalls. First, using personal material can be narcissistic, making the actors look inward, at themselves. This can turn rehearsal into group therapy, which is usually fatal to good theatre. The point of theatre is not to stop at analysis but to communicate to the audience. You need to create distance between the actors and their material. For example, get the actors to play each other rather than themselves.

Second, you have a problem if the writer, director and actor and source material are all the same person. In conventional theatre the script passes from the writer to the producer, to director and designers, and finally to the actors who give it to the audience. At each stage the script is criticized and revised by each professional eye that examines it. You need to give workshop performances and invite professional friends not connected with the production to come to see the work in progress. The aim is to generate critical discussion. Even if this doesn't happen the actors themselves, if they are any good, will know in their gut if something is wrong as soon as they get in front of the audience.

EMPATHY WITH OTHERS

Actors can create theatre from the lives and experiences of others. They work empathetically with their subjects, adopting their point of view. Peter Cheesman's celebrated experiment at Stoke in the late 1970s involved his theatre in the fight to save the steel foundry at Shelton Bar. Actors were paired with individual steelworkers in the workplace. Their job was to 'become' these steelworkers, creating a document of life at the steelworks. The actors, being of similar age to the workers, had much in common with the people they were portraying. A powerful empathic documentary resulted, with theatre at the heart of an issue of great local importance. The community became involved with the show, which consisted of sketches, documentary and song. It developed and new material added as the situation developed at the steelworks. Steelworkers stood up in the audience at the end of the show to bring the audience absolutely up to date with latest developments. The show evolved as events developed. Part of the rehearsal took place at the steelworks, where each actor researched the routines, actions and motivations of the individual worker they were shadowing. They became empathetically involved with the person they were going to portray on stage. In the rehearsal room, the material was

- Don't try to say everything: be highly selective.
- Concentrate on all points of change. If a person changes, changes someone else or is changed by events, these are 'dramatic' moments of interest to an audience. Documentary account alone is of no relevance to theatre.
- Shape the material to your dramatic purpose. You are making theatre, not a news broadcast. You are allowed to exaggerate, emphasize a pattern you have found in a story, compress the narrative, leave out events, alter the sequence, change the timescale, convert and alter material.
- As the material takes shape as theatre rather than narrative, become sensitive to style. Does it feel expressionistic, like a series of emotional flashes? Surreal/dreamlike? Realistic, as though you were overhearing a conversation?
- Consider delivering some material as song, poetry, storytelling or movement.

tested for its dramatic value and shaped for entertainment and audience engagement.

The creation of theatre from true-life stories offers a wide range of possibilities. Living history projects with senior citizens are possible, and issue-based projects in which profile and shape might be given to the lives of a group of immigrants, or individuals re-entering the community from an institution.

Actors can shadow subjects and use their stories or writing to create a text. Character and plot are alive and in front of the actor. A successful model, like Shelton Bar, builds the subject into the theatre so that rather than being used, subjects are in partnership with the actors.

Gathering material is usually a pre-rehearsal task. Devising rehearsals concentrate on turning narrative into dramatic material.

WORKING FROM CHARACTER

Mike Leigh created theatre and then film scripts by rehearsing individually with actors to create characters based on actors' observation of real people. Once the actors have 'become' these individual characters, they are brought together in 'real' encounters. Leigh writes scripts from these improvisations (*see* Coveney in Bibliography).

The possibilities for devised shows from characters are infinite. One-person shows and devised shows from historical characters are common. Research to create such characters will vary according to the historical period and the occupation of the subject. Victorian characters, for example, are often letter-writing diarists and the actor is liable to be drowned in material. With a character like Shakespeare, however, of whom nothing significant is known, the task involves intuitive construction and creative decision-making. The object is always to find the human connection between the character and modern human beings. We are not writing biography, but bringing someone to life. The risk in rehearsal is filling the show with banal biographical material while neglecting the moments that reveal the common humanity of the character. Audiences are drawn to historical characters, not to discover facts about them, but to have light thrown on their own nature and being.

It is fun and exciting to conjure up imaginative characters from the past and present from props. Visit junk shops and car boot sales. Find someone's pipe or scarf or make-up compact. Imagine and visualize the owner. Decide their age, station and occupation. Hunt like a detective for other possessions or bits of evidence that throw light on this imaginative character. Find their photograph. Begin to create their

Physicalizing the plot of World of George Orwell.

biography. This sort of activity should be the actor's everyday work.

WORKING FROM STORIES

Mike Alfreds formed 'Shared Experience' in 1975, to explore the roots of live theatre. Alfreds and the company developed a comprehensive system that trod the line between storytelling and theatre. The actor-narrators directly address the audience, while stepping in and out of dialogue, which was written as speech in the original prose. The resulting highly dramatic text left the original story severely edited but stylistically intact. Following great success with *Arabian Nights*, the company transposed a range of novels. The fashion for adapting nineteenth-century novels that followed is now almost played out, but the acting technique of storytelling remains a powerful devising tool.

The form has worked most successfully for 'epic' stories – expansive tales often spanning several generations and whole continents. The flexibility of storytelling technique lends itself to this form. Actors can narrate passing aeons, treks across the world, and fantastic battles. By contrast, passages of dialogue can be lifted verbatim from the original story to create vibrant emotional moments between the characters.

The narrator-actor has a particular relationship with the audience. There is directness, an intimacy and something akin to a real relationship, which develops as the story unfolds. A skilled actor can manipulate this relationship, and it is useful to rehearse before an active audience, so that this living communication can be practised along with the scenario.

DECONSTRUCTION

Deconstruction is a way of using a text – often a classic text – as a kick-start to a devised theatre piece. It is not an adaptation, but an original piece of theatre inspired by a conventional script. Useful plays are those that have wonderful flashes in them – a great scene or theme, or some wonderful characters – which are either deeply flawed, dated or impractical to do in their original state. Take such a play to pieces, preserving what you find irresistible. Then apply your own creative input, possibly other material, or your own writing, and create a new piece of theatre as a response to the

The team writes scene titles on cards and negotiates running order.

original. Usually the play you started with is not recognizable in the finished product, so the source is not very important, except that it inspires something in you that speaks to the contemporary world.

Stage 1

Take a play, or a sequence of scenes, or a single scene, and dissect it. Examples of dissections might include:

* Describe the plot in four or five headings.
* Create a single title for the piece.
* Draw a table of the plotline and the sub-plots. Draw a picture of the relationship between the plot and sub-plots.
* Map the relationships and draw a diagram of the relationship dynamics.
* Characterize the 'world' of the piece. Is it youthful or old? Idealistic or cynical? Dark or light? Of love or war? Materialistic or spiritual? And so on.
* List the themes, for example ambition, incest, boardroom politics, unrequited love, jealousy.
* Indicate the politics of the piece.
* List the irresistible qualities of the piece. Make this list utterly arbitrary: qualities, character traits, snatches of speech, stage directions; anything that appeals.

Stage 2

Create physical shapes out of the prevailing themes. Dance the piece. You are chewing it up until its shape has gone. Find other ways to cut up the play. Each cut you make is a potential kick-start to a devised theatre piece.

Stage 3

You now reconstruct not the original play but your own piece. The process combines analysis and intuition, depending upon what you want to say and what draws you to the piece. You might consider using shift of focus, displacement, personalization or form and framework.

World of George Orwell *dress run for touring production.*

Shift of Focus

Choose an element from your cuttings that, while not central to the original play, strongly appeals to you as the focus of the reconstructed piece. Use other elements of your deconstruction and your own additions to highlight this element in your piece. Your focus might be a character, relationship or political theme, or anything that stirs your imagination as the seed of a theatre piece.

Displacement

Transfer any element of the original piece, for example the characters or relationship between two characters, to a different culture, time or place. Follow through all of the implications of this transposition. Let it affect the entire world of the new piece.

Personalization

Use personal material as an additional element to the process. Record your reactions and responses to the play, the personal material that the play draws from you. Consider creating 'then and now' flashbacks if the original play is historically set.

Form and Framework

Consider a number of possible frameworks for the reconstruction. Your options might be collage, in which different 'cuts' are juxtaposed to give a vibrant theatrical impression. Epic storytelling interspersed with scene playing is another possibility. Stage poem is an option, which creates a 'living art' response to the original. There are less extreme options, which are more like adaptations of the original than the creation of original pieces.

You can do what you like, so long as it speaks to an audience! Above all, let this process be playful. Play is the only state in which you are likely to stumble on the unexpected. When the process becomes clerical, you will be wasting your time, so stop, have a break or carry on working at another part of the job.

THEATRE WITHOUT PLAYWRIGHTS

Unless playwriting is of special interest to the company, avoid long writing sessions, which often kill the company's creative energy. Action, rather than planning or reflecting, comes most naturally to the actor, and a devising company rarely has the rehearsal time to write a play. If the company consists of well-trained craft actors, directors can rely upon them to be able to repeat what they have done. This is the mark of a professional actor, and devising directors should test this skill when auditioning the cast.

Developing Material without Playwrighting

Using skilled actors, it would be possible to develop the material in the following way:

1. Select improvisation themes from the source material.
2. Begin by running long exploratory improvisations. Be patient, allow the actors to explore the theme, don't expect immediate results, but note every theatrical or dramatic moment that arises.
3. The director works from notes to compress the material, putting together dramatic moments gleaned from the exploratory impros and creating little sequences that can be summarized in brief headings.
4. Actors now improvise scenes of no more than one minute using these headings.
5. Improvisations are repeated. Actors practise creating and re-creating dramatic moments into a short scene.
6. The material is refined through repetition and notes are made as subheadings between the director's main headings, creating a little list of cues.
7. The actor can then refine the scene by further repetition, using the notes as a series of cues.
8. Late in the process, it may be possible to write up the scene. The quickest way to do this is to get the actors to write out their own parts with the preceding cue line. This is called a 'side'.
9. The director could photocopy and paste up the parts as a finished script.

If a video recorder is available it can be invaluable, but it should be used sparingly and in conjunction with the notes. If you record yards of video or audiotape you won't use it, because you won't have time to plough through it to find the piece you want, so video or audio tape should be heavily edited and used as a reference tool.

Apart from the audio and videotape, Elizabethan actors would probably have been perfectly at home with this process.

FACILITATING WORKSHOPS – THE GROUP PROCESS

The group as a whole – the company – is a personality in its own right. Like a person, it can have 'on' and 'off' days, it can have moods and it needs different stimulation and boundaries at different times. It also needs time on its own, away from the director. Furthermore, it may be quite different in character if even one of its members is missing. Avoid making an issue out of this, but take the group process into consideration as well as the devising process when planning your next step. A model for this parallel process of groupwork and theatremaking might look something like that shown on the table opposite.

WRITING ON YOUR FEET

You might wish to create scenes, dialogue and stage directions, since the issue of scene writing is sometimes unavoidable in a devised production. Try nevertheless to allow actors to

Devising Process

Rehearsal Stage	Director's Task	State of Company Group Dynamic	Director's Role
First and early rehearsals	To facilitate verbal and physical communication between individual actors	The group hasn't yet formed Individuals negotiate with each other for roles, cliques form	Director as the *channel of communication* between all members of the company
Early rehearsals	To communicate the 'big picture' – the vision for the project	Individuals gain a sense of belonging to the project	Director *leads* the group from the centre
Early workshops	To facilitate 'success in small things' To witness achievement, and affirm growth, building the group's confidence in itself	Individuals establish genuine relationships through work The character of the group begins to show Work ethic established	Director as an enthusiastic, committed and forward-driving partner, a group *role model*
Creating the material	To establish and manage a timetable of work .	Individual actors or sub-groups devise a system for creating material	Director as *manager* and work co-ordinator
Creating the material	To foster and operate a culture of creative criticism	Individual or sub-groups present to the company and revise work in progress	Director as creative negotiator and *decision-taker*
Shaping the material	To run workshops and rehearsals To meet the acting, technical and skill requirements of the developing scenario	The company maintains a strong sense of identity through 'whole company' work The company gains ownership of the work	Director as diagnostic session leader
Shaping the material	To create links and devise a holding form for the material created by the company and the production and design teams	Director negotiates individual roles in the theatre piece, with the company, having regard to their shared vision	Director as *theatre maker*
Delivering the production	To function as a detached, expert observer	Company consolidates around the common task	Director as *ideal audience*
Delivering the production	To focus the relationship between the design and production teams, with the acting group, creating a whole company from all of these	Company becomes increasingly autonomous in anticipation of performance – responsive to, but independent of the director	Role of *artistic director*

A moment to reflect and revise.

remain actors during this process. Don't make them sit down with a pen if you can avoid it. You can use shadowing for conventional work with a script, or as a devising technique. A possible framework is as follows:

1. Work in pairs. Each actor is accompanied by a 'shadow'. The actor speaks and moves as the character, the shadow follows the actor, suggesting words to say and things to do.
2. Begin with physical actions only. The shadow simply gives the actor stage directions. The shadow might say 'You enter the room, look round ... see her, smile and look away. Walk to the window' ... and so on. The actor does as he or she is told.
3. Add words. The shadow feeds words and actions to their actor partner. The idea is that

the shadow takes care of the writing and the actor plays out the instructions as fully as possible. When using text the shadow functions as a very attentive prompter. The actor is freed to move physically and this is very important at the beginning of scene rehearsal, when actors must avoid rehearsing tension into themselves as they wrestle with the text.
4. You can adapt this basic framework to suit your needs. For example, the shadows can sit as an 'audience' and prompt the actor, or they can work very close to their actors, even moving them physically. The actor can only respond to the shadow's instructions, or add to those instructions, or the shadow can make no suggestions until the actor asks for them.

84

9 A TEXT REHEARSAL

TEXT IS NOT LITERATURE

A playtext is not literature. Shakespeare's friends had a great struggle after his death to get the Bodleian Library to accept his plays, and many no doubt excellent Elizabethan plays ended in the bin because no respectable library would give them a home. The Bodleian accepted poetry, essays, treatises and tracts – literature, in fact – but not plays. In 1616 it knew that playwrights were like wheelwrights and cartwrights. A play, like a cart or a wheel, was wrought, that is, crafted from different elements, with a greater or lesser degree of skill. Text was not literature. Text was not even literature read out loud, in spite of the best efforts of the Victorians.

So what is text? Text is a blueprint for action, and it is the most specific and detailed blueprint imaginable. A well-seasoned play – one that has been worked over by thorough actors and revised by a craft writer – has no fat on it. It is only action, and the words are the tip of the iceberg of action, which will emerge during rehearsal. A great text yields copious material at every level. Characterization, storyline, movement, style, manners, social mores, indeed the entire 'world' of the play, can all be found in its language. Actors need considerable technique and experience to completey embody a good text, and a director needs the same to bring it to life.

Text, Action and Activities

When you are directing text, your job throughout rehearsal is to encourage the actor away from recitation towards action. The best advice on how to do this was given by Stanislavski who, frustrated at trying to evoke and extinguish emotion in actors by direct means, turned to indirect methods. He invited the actor to analyse a scene according to objectives, that is, according to what the character seeks to gain from the action of the play. Objectives consist of many 'actions', and an 'action' refers to what a character wants in any given moment. The convention is that all characters want something all the time. They want to get something from the other characters, or get them to do something, or to manipulate them in some way. If you get what you want, says Stanislavski (I paraphrase) then positive feelings result. However, if some obstacle defeats your want, you feel negative. The obstacle could be an outer obstacle, for example, your want may have to change or be adjusted because of another character's want (counteraction). Alternatively, an inner obstacle could block your want – your conscience, for example. Actions, counteractions and obstacles produce dramatic conflict within the scene, or sometimes within the characters themselves. Feelings don't have to be 'acted' – they arise naturally from getting or losing objectives so long as the actor doesn't shut those feelings off. The director's work in connecting the actor to the text is to encourage in the actor the idea that no one in a play talks just for the sake of it. Characters in a scene have wants – not what they say they want, but the underlying motivation that drives them from moment to moment.

THE LIFE OF THE TEXT

Your job as director is to 'midwife' the play through the rehearsal process, first by bringing it to life, then by nourishing and strengthening it – preventing it from going unconscious and dying on you, then by stepping away to watch it grow on its own.

The First Rehearsal

Unless you are working with a well-seasoned team, don't read through at the first rehearsal. The actors will do what you tell them of course, but they may be too preoccupied with surviving the social encounters and newness of the situation to absorb information. The readthrough, as the company's first collective encounter with the text, is a seminal rehearsal, so do anything but read through on a first meeting – improvise on a theme, play a game session, let people talk to each other and find out who they are working with. There's a lot to be said for a session in the pub. If you need to start work on the play immediately, take a key scene or a theme and use the rehearsal to improvise and open up a discussion about the world of the play. However, if you can hold off, you may find that not reading through at the first rehearsal creatively disconcerts your actors. To most actors, read-through leads to discussion, blocking, memorizing, run-throughs, dress rehearsal and performance. Once they feel themselves on the tramlines of their expectations they will sometimes put their creativity to sleep while they coast through the process. Although I am going to follow this path in describing a text rehearsal, any appropriate deviation from this well-trodden route wakes up the actors and puts them on their mettle while they wrestle with the invigorating discomfort of an unexpected situation.

First Readthrough

Experienced actors will know how to use this seminal and vital rehearsal, but those less experienced will need direction, because often in early rehearsals avoiding making a mistake is more important than receiving information.

As director you must explain your vision for the production, but don't speak for more than five minutes at the start, unless you want to establish an unspoken rule that you speak and they listen. If you want the company to join in, get to the readthrough as soon as possible, but stop frequently as issues arise, fill out your vision of the production and respond to comments and questions.

How do you want people to read? The answer will tell actors a lot about your style as a director. Some directors ask for a 'flat' reading with no expression. They wish the actor to come to the text with no preconceptions, ready to be totally directed. Others will ask for communication. Actors are encouraged to look at, speak to and respond to each other on a first reading. Other directors may even indicate characterization or other 'try outs' at first rehearsal. There is no correct way to start, but think it through carefully, because in deciding your approach you are indicating your relationship with the actors and setting out the culture of the rehearsal room.

Take notes, and encourage others to do so. First readings with the whole company reveal the play most sharply to the senses. The twists of the storyline, the oddness and brilliance of the plot, meeting the characters for the first time, the greatness or the faults of the imagery all contribute to the 'taste' of the text. Discovery and discussion with others is at its sharpest at the first encounter. Within a couple of rehearsals you will be using the play like an old sock, all sensation smoothed out by the habit of rehearsal. Then you will want to recapture those initial sensations and you will need your notes.

Improvising Themes and Issues

The word 'drama' means 'doing', so try to break up your early discussions by trying things out. It's much easier to discuss something you've

First readthrough.

A Parallel Improvisation – *Romeo and Juliet*

Theme selected by the director: Adolescent love in the world of adults.

Parallel Improvisation
A formal dinner party, one family hosted by the other. The lovers may only speak freely when alone; otherwise, they must behave as polite strangers. The adults create windows of opportunity for the lovers by finding reasons to withdraw or send them away, but re-intervene at will, breaking the flow of their emotional contact.

Thematic Explorations
• The two families ignore their enmity for the purposes of the impro, and are therefore free to explore what they have in common as parents.

• The lovers create together the secret world of freely expressed feeling.
• The company explores the rituals of formal society and of personal relationship.
• The lovers devise and create their own language of love.

Exercise
Using *Romeo and Juliet*, devise parallel impros around the following themes:

• Brothers (Romeo's friends) and fathers (the fathers and governors of Verona).
• Infatuation and death.
• Love and sectarian hatred.

done, rather than something you might do. The latter is full of worries and fantasies, while the former is the simple development of a piece of work. While discussion is a vital rehearsal tool, it must be used appropriately, and not as a way of avoiding getting onto your feet.

Simple 'parallel improvisations' are appropriate at this stage. Take a theme that is fundamental to your view of the play and create a situation in which the actors can explore it. The situation you suggest should be very familiar to the actors, and the improvisation very simple, so that all energy can focus on the designated theme. Play through the impro a couple of times with no more direction than is absolutely necessary to focus on the material you wish to explore. You will find that after improvising, the actors will be able to discuss the theme from experience rather than in theory.

Working the Script

When you start scene rehearsals, explore with the actors what the characters are doing to each other in the scene. If you can underpin the text with clear action, you will start to bring the scene to life. Your purpose is to help the actor to connect with the scene at gut, rather than at head, level.

Take a scene or a piece of a scene and define the characters' actions (see 'Text, Actions and Activities' on page 85). What does she want/want to do to/want from him? How does he want to change/move/manipulate her? Encourage the actor to choose transitive actions. If the actor can't turn the 'action' words into a physical gesture then it will not be much use, because they want that gesture inside them as they speak the words. Obviously the text must justify the choice of action. The action word or phrase is vitally important – it must affect the actor at gut level. Whatever the final choice, actors must choose something they can play.

For example, suppose you are working with two actors and choosing actions for a scene that is a moment in a love affair. 'To get him/her to go out with me' isn't a very transitive action. It is bland: neither physical nor immediate. 'To seduce him' is much better. It gives you something to do! And it is more 'now'.

You might decide to choose a more abstract but still transitive image, for example an elemental image of earth, air, fire or water: 'To set him on fire' might work, or 'To drown her in love.' You might choose a simple physical action. Actions like 'To send him away' or 'To keep her in the room' might work because they are simple, immediate gestures.

When you have defined actions appropriate to the text, choose some activities or tactics. You know what you want but how are you going to get it? By pleading, bullying, shaming, coaxing, forcing? Perhaps more than one tactic; perhaps you change tactics.

When each actor has developed a little pattern of actions and tactics appropriate to their character in the scene, they put the text down and broadly improvise the scene or scene section by strongly playing the actions. They make up what words they need, letting the words follow the actions. When working the text, the actors don't bother with characterization at all – that is different work and can come separately. Repeat the impro two or three times until it takes on a shape and the actors begin to gain a little confidence and freedom.

Now the actors pick up the text and speak the text on their feet, reading the text but playing the actions and tactics strongly, as they did before. If the play is any good, the precision of the language and the physical commitment of the actor will produce a powerful moment.

Now you have something to discuss! Alter, refine, improvise better and more specific actions, develop the action that underlies the words.

Beat to Beat

For our purposes a beat is period of time in a scene containing a set of continuous actions, or

Working the text. Note that stage management have marked the set on the floor.

Example: *All My Sons* by Arthur Miller

Scene: Act 2, Kate Kellor's (Joe's wife's) second entrance.

Setting: George has returned to confront Joe Kellor, whom he believes was guilty of shipping faulty cylinder heads to the US air force and allowing George's father to be convicted and imprisoned for the crime.

George's objective:	*To force* Joe Kellor to face his guilt.
George's action:	*To break* the mould of his relationship with the Kellors.
George's tactics:	*To transform* himself (he wears a hat for the first time).
	To undermine his sister's confidence in the Kellors.
	To provoke a confrontation with Chris Kellor.
	To resist Kate Kellor.
Kate Kellor's objective:	*To hold* her family together.
Kate's (counter)action:	*To castrate* George as a potent threat to her 'truth'.
Kate's tactics:	*To trigger* the 'little boy' he was when they last met.
	To smother him with affection.
	To feed him with food, and with her view of the world.

When rehearsal goes well, it continues on another level through the breaks.

the part of a scene characterized by a single mood or atmosphere. A beat has a particular emotional colour. A beat might last for a number of scenes or there might be several in a scene. The director might prepare a scene by dividing it into beats, by marking the emotional or atmospheric changes that occur in the scene as a whole, rather than in the individual characters. Individual characters may or may not be in tune with the atmosphere of a beat, so the director should go through the scene with the actors, agreeing the precise moments in a given scene when the beat changes. Once these are clear and the actors are familiar with, and have played through, their actions, you can begin to work beat to beat.

Play the scene through, asking the actors to stop and all say 'beat' together at each point of change. You might ask the actors to make a physical shape that expresses the atmosphere of the next beat at each point of change. The object is to work with the actor's body and impulses, rather than their head. During this phase, actors learn that although their actions are played against each other, they are simultaneously co-operating to give the scene shape.

Blocking

Blocking means telling people where to stand, and sometimes what gestures to make. There are directors who block everything very early, and then drill their actors. Actors then 'justify' the blocking; that is, they do their best to make it human. Technicalities of blocking are discussed on page 46.

If you work using beats you will not need to block scenes that have four or less actors in them. If the actors understand their intentions they will move naturally round the stage. Your 'ideal audience eye' will pass over the scene and, quite late in the rehearsal process, you will simply have to indicate to the actors points at which they must adjust to favour the audience, or where they could be making shapes that better indicate their intentions. However, you must block when you have a crowd onstage. In this case, improvise or read through and move the scene until you can note the start and the finish pattern of the bodies onstage, and maybe one or two interesting moments in between. Stop the rehearsal and take your time to record the pattern. Don't let the artificiality of the moment phase you. All art is artificial.

Announce your blocking rehearsal and let the actors know that nothing is expected of them except to record their moves. They will relax, you will have time to do your job, and you can create a 'script' of the moves in the given scene.

Learning Lines

If the actors know what they are doing it won't take them long to learn lines. If actors regularly stumble over particular passages, there might be some deeper problem of comprehension. There is a stage in rehearsal when the technicalities of the text get in the way of expression. Rehearsals will have gone very smoothly 'on the book', the actors appearing to have an emotional and physical grasp of their lines. Once the books are put down, however, all the previous work seems to disappear because the actors immediately retreat into their heads, trying to 'get things right'. Actors in thought rather than in action once more confront the director.

It is important to give the actor space at this point in the sense that you are prepared to go more slowly, repeat sequences and sometimes work to the actor's competence rather than to the finished rhythm of the piece. On the other hand it is very important that you continue to give notes all through this 'remembering' period, however uncomfortable it is for the actor. You may get signals intended to warn you off giving notes or intervening while the actor resolves the technical problem of lines-in-action, but it is fatal to give in to this. Remember that the actor is always transforming towards the performance. There is no neutral position –

91

the actor is either learning it right or learning it wrong, so in the course of accommodating the text, or any technicality, all sorts of bad habits can be unconsciously learned unless you carefully and immediately weed them out.

The Last Lap: Keeping the Text Alive to the End

Once the action of the play has been mapped, the company has shaped it beat by beat, and the actor has integrated the text with the action, you will want to connect up the rehearsal sections into acts and finally the whole play. It is important to 'run' as early as possible because the actors get a sense of the world of the play and their character's place in it, by experiencing the whole thing. Some actors take great strides during run-throughs. Consider readthroughs, walkthroughs and playthroughs throughout the rehearsal process.

RIGHT: *Nic Tudor giving notes.*
BELOW: *Note the set and acting space mocked up in the rehearsal room.*

Once you have come to your final runs, you have two apparently contradictory jobs. The first is to revisit your vision of the play, and to

establish through repetition and adjustment the overall shape of the production. The second is to keep the play alive, moment by moment, for the actors. Unless there is an edge of spontaneity in the playing, no degree of 'correctness' will bring the production to life.

Intersperse your runs with scene rehearsals in which you create 'points of focus' for the actor, which may or may not relate to the actual context of the scene in the play. For example, play the scene as though in pouring rain, full of desire for each other, as though late for an appointment, and so on. The point of focus is entirely arbitrary, but its purpose is to challenge the speech patterns that the actor is unconsciously repeating. The point of focus connects at arbitrary points in the scene, giving it resonance. Choose 'opposite characteristics' for your characters to remind actors of concealed, rejected, or 'shadow' qualities in the character. For example:

- Play Juliet as though she were a brazen whore, trying to pick up Romeo.
- Play Henry V as though he were Hamlet.
- Play Lady Macbeth as a deranged suburban housewife trying to get her life together.
- Play King Lear as though he were Richard III.
- Play Falstaff as though he were Iago.

An Important Reminder

The rehearsal process, like all living things, is rarely textbook perfect. It is quite normal to stop and start again, not to slavishly follow the logical order of rehearsal, and to change your mind. When everything goes smoothly, when there are no disagreements or heated differences, or insurmountable blocks, it may be because no one cares passionately about the production decisions. Then you do have problems!

That's it. If you have not integrated your design, sound, lights, costume and music into the process, you will begin to work them into the picture at this point (see Chapter 5).

THE WORLD OF THE PLAYWRIGHT: SOME NOTES ON STYLE

Great playwrights create an imaginative world distinct to themselves, however many and various their plays. Directors must develop a clear picture of the rules and conventions employed by the playwright before they start work with the actors. They can then decide whether to stay consistently within them or to break or comment on them. Here are a few brief notes on the 'worlds' of four playwrights who have had a massive effect on contemporary theatre.

Shakespeare
Shakespeare's characters live a symbolic life in which their thoughts and actions move smoothly backwards and forwards from the domestic and mundane, to the heavens, the actions of kings and princes, and to the mythological fates of gods. Symbolic action is achieved through poetic imagery. Shakespeare uses iambic pentameter, a verse form very near to the rhythm of human speech, but capable of carrying heightened poetic sensibilities.

Shakespeare uses symbolic conventions in characterization. For example, Richard III's deformed body reflects his deformed soul. Only kings and princes speak in iambic pentameter; the 'lower orders' use prose and usually inhabit a comic world in contrast to the potentially tragic world of kings.

When considering the actions of Shakespeare's women, remember that in his time an adult woman had the simple choice of becoming a wife, a nun or a prostitute.

There is no subtext in Shakespeare. Characters who are going to lie to or deceive someone will usually walk downstage and tell the audience. In fact everything on the Shakespearean stage is done or said in the presence of the audience, so it is natural sometimes for characters to speak to it. Shutting out the audience or pretending there is a 'fourth wall' between actor and audience is always a mistake.

Brecht

Almost all of Brecht's plays are teaching plays. There is a strong element of demonstration and storytelling. Brecht wished to demonstrate that human nature is not fixed, but changes according to circumstances. 'Change the circumstances and you change the person' is a strong argument for revolutionary social change, and a strong characterization indicator for the actor.

Brecht admired Shakespeare and adapted a number of Elizabethan plays. He liked their 'no tricks, no illusions' style of theatre.

The concept of *Verfremdung* or 'alienation', sometimes called by its French name *distantiation*, gives directors and actors a lot of problems. Alienation is simply a way of reminding the audience that they are in a theatre, and that they are watching a point of view, not 'the truth'. Breaking into song, picking up and reading from the text, using verse, and artificial lighting changes, are techniques designed to break the sometimes hypnotic effect of watching the play and re-engage the audience's capacity for argument.

Many of Brecht's innovations have been absorbed into conventional practice. Lighting the audience, exposing the theatre lanterns, actors dressing and making up on stage, the use of puppetry, radio and film, the use of Chinese theatre conventions and acting technique, revolutionary for their time, are now part of mainstream theatre practice.

Checkov

Checkov's world is intimate. He wanted you to feel as though you were seated in a café, overhearing an intimate conversation at the table next to you.

In Checkov everyone lies about their feelings; the real action of the play is in the subtext. This is the world of feeling beneath the world of words, and the feelings do not lie. The dynamic tension between these worlds in individuals and between characters creates the dramatic action of the play.

Although Checkov's theatre is realistic, it is not simply a slice of life dumped onto the stage. Checkov's plays are quite unnatural. There is a great deal of symbolism and the action is hugely compressed.

Feydeau

Feydeau writes farce, but Feydeau's farces are dark and sometimes frightening, which makes them models for modern political farceurs such as Dario Fo.

Farce has to move at great speed. If it slows down, the ludicrousness of the plot is immediately exposed. Trousers must be pulled up exactly as doors are opened and vicars must shut themselves into the wardrobe an instant before the enraged husband bursts into the bedroom.

Farce is highly technical. You need all practical props and every bit of the practical set – windows, doors and cupboard – that are used very early in rehearsal. If you can't, mock up everything that the actors have to use. You must mechanically block each moment of the play. The plays are full of stage business, which must be set early and rehearsed thoroughly. Actors must hit their marks as though they were in a film and they must bring your mechanical blocking to life.

The point is that the characters don't actually know that they are in a farce. Unlike the audience, they don't know the whole circumstances of their situation. We, the audience, know more than they do so we laugh at them. Farce is as cruel as bear-baiting, though in farce the audience always feels that blood is about to be drawn.

PART THREE

REHEARSAL ADVICE
TO ACTORS

Peter Brook describes two types of good director. One is clear and purposeful: actors know they can rely on him. The other is clearly useless: actors know immediately that the production will depend entirely on them. The dangerous director, says Brook, is the one whose uselessness is not apparent until it is too late to save the production.

Good directors know how to motivate their actors, some by driving them, some by eliciting their help. For their part, good actors must act, not only on stage but by being active collaborators and contributors to the rehearsal process, even when production values and directional decisions are not to their taste.

The final part of this book concentrates on the actor rehearsing out of or between formal rehearsals. The actor has clear responsibilities to the creative collaboration: making stage sense of the text and creating a full and believable character consistent with the world of the play. Trying out ideas and developing relationships and stage partnership with fellow actors is also a vital element of rehearsal that does not require the presence of the director. Finally, what does the actor do when 'resting' and there is nothing to rehearse? The actor who is a truly active artist will develop a work pattern in which it is possible to get up each morning and start work, either alone or with professional associates. It is this independent-minded actor, capable of creating and performing, who has the best chance of long-term success.

10 THE IMPROVISING ACTOR

WHY DIRECTORS PLAY GAMES AND IMPROVISE

If rehearsal is not to be a form of surgery, with the director setting precise tasks to be precisely met by the actor within the rigid frame of the director's vision, then some playing will be necessary, if only to leaven the incredibly hard work of producing a play. All of the exercises suggested in this book are types of improvisation. However, this chapter concentrates on exercises and games that help to warm up the actor's spontaneous side and develop that 'in the moment' attitude that is alert, listening and responding, and not too frightened to get it wrong. It is important to get these juices running as well as to warm up the voice and body. Modern actors must be able to take improvisation in their stride, since it is an important aspect of rehearsal and is likely to feature at audition.

Company Style

Improvisation is sometimes the company style. The company creates and rehearses plays through improvisation and seeks a particular sort of actor, who will be compatible with the company in terms of their attitude and professional working methods. The director will test this during audition. The ability to be flexible, responsive and at ease with impro will be as important to this sort of company as casting considerations.

Diagnosis and Treatment of Rehearsal Problems

Sometimes it is necessary to step sideways in rehearsal and work around a problem or obstacle that is blocking the progress of the work. Impro and games are useful for freeing up situations that have become 'locked'. Games and impro can free up a rehearsal, helping it to become active and physical. Most directors use a relatively small vocabulary of games and exercises, and many take a diagnostic approach and proceed conventionally unless there is some practical need to improvise. Others use impro as an aspect of research, either using it between the early readthroughs and the blocking stage of rehearsal to develop a production style, or employing it in the many ways described in Chapter 7. On the other hand, some directors are scared of impro and won't use it at all. This is perfectly acceptable, but if you are an actor who likes to work through games and impro and you need to play, there's nothing to stop you using this chapter to do your own sessions when not called for rehearsal.

Fashion

There are good and bad directors, and the latter will sometimes play around and waste your time because they don't know what to do next, or because they wish to be thought experimental. This can be confusing and actors should resist the temptation to mystify the director's process.

Oedipus, about to blind himself, improvises for the last time with sunlight.

Good directors will make the rehearsal objectives clear to the actor. If they get lost they will say so, since 'lost' is a perfectly acceptable place to be. If you find yourself working with someone who can't direct traffic, take what you can from the rehearsal, and quietly get on with rehearsing on your own and with colleagues as best you can. Don't make the mistake of projecting onto the director mysterious powers beyond your understanding. If you can't see the point, ask.

SKILLS AND ATTITUDES

Just as there are non-improvising directors, there are also non-improvising actors. Improvisation involves giving up control, tolerating mess and enjoying thrashing around in the dark. Not everyone is suited to this, and unless you are doing Stanislavski's improvisations the process is rarely logical or methodological. Also you and the director need time and space to improvise and to reflect on what emerges from the impros, and this is not always available. Actors who enjoy improvisation can do this work together outside of formal scene rehearsal time and treat impro as research, which is what it is.

The root of improvisation is playfulness, which nearly all of us understand because play is the business of childhood. This means that anyone can have a go at improvisation if they accept that it is a state of mind – an attitude rather than a skill. Some improvisers are more skilled than others, but actors do not need to be highly skilled, only willing to explore, have a go and see what happens.

Anyone who wants to develop his or her improvisation skills should read Keith Johnstone's book *Impro – Improvisation and the Theatre*. Johnstone wrote this book in the sixties and now affects to dislike it. Its value, however, lies not only in the exercises but in its approach to creative learning, and especially to the way young artists grow and learn.

Warming Up Alone

Open Face, Open Body

First warm up your face by increasing the blood flow to it. Rub lightly over your scalp and down either side of your nose. Close your eyes and gently place the heels of your palms over your eyelids and stroke outwards. Rub the flat of your hand backwards and forwards across your mouth. Put your first and second fingers behind your ears and massage lightly by rubbing up and down. Pinch around the edges and lobes of your ears until they tingle. Rub the back of your hand backwards and forwards under your chin.

When you have warmed up your face and it is tingling, stretch the muscles:

1. Make your face as long as possible.
2. Make it as flat as possible.
3. Pinch it in, as though you were sucking a lemon.
4. Make it as big and wide as you can.

Now look into a mirror. Open your eyes wider than normal, but not so wide that it shows. You will feel that they are opening long before anyone else notices. Do the same with your mouth – make it a little wider than normal. Speak your speeches with the sensation that your eyes and mouth are a little larger than usual. Use this little exercise as an impro warm-up; have a conversation using this sensation. The feeling that your eyes and mouth are slightly larger than usual will give you the biofeedback that makes you feel warmer, bigger, more generous.

Stream of Words, Stream of Gestures

Point to anything in the room and say its name. Do the same to object after object until you are speaking a smooth stream of words. Repeat until you can do this without hesitation. You need a relaxed frame of mind, so don't try too hard. You are practising speaking without thinking, without censoring yourself.

Next do the same exercise, but say the wrong name. Work for a stream of words. Now do the original exercise but move around the room, reacting to the object with large gestures. You are aiming for the sense that each object affects you as you name it. You are playing with the idea of 'yielding' to impulses.

The idea of this whole sequence is to make the objects in the room resonate in your imagination.

Tragi-Comic

Make a large, expansive gesture that involves your whole body. Work on it a little until it has a shape: a beginning, a middle and an end.

Now work on it to give it a 'tragic' feel and then, without changing the shape of the gesture, work

Triggering an impro by physicalizing a relationship.

OPPOSITE PAGE
Using a 'sensing' gesture to trigger an impro.

on it to give it a comic feel. If working with someone else, or others, 'give' someone else your tragic gesture and let them re-create it in a comic form. Lastly, add sounds to your gesture.

Avoid clichés; make the choice dramatic, perhaps based on a character, and work for complete involvement. You are rehearsing concentration, physical tempo, rhythm and gesture as an expression of inner feeling.

Warming Up with a Partner
Saying 'Yes'
Saying 'Yes!' is what makes improvisers different and more dangerous than ordinary people. In life, if someone walks up to us with a proposition we are inclined to say 'No thanks', 'I'll think about it' or 'Maybe'. Improvisers say 'Yes' immediately, and because they are on stage and not in real life, they don't have to pay for saying 'Yes'. However, it feels strange to say 'Yes' all the time, so you need to practise.

Exercise 1 – 'Yes'
Your partner asks you a succession of questions to which you have to answer 'yes'. The questions invite you to transform physically. For example:

1st actor: 'Is it cold?'
2nd actor: 'Yes' (starts to shiver).
1st: 'And are you very fat?'
2nd: 'Yes' (becomes fat and keeps shivering).
1st: 'Are you a giant penguin?'
2nd: 'Yes' (becomes one).
1st: 'At the North Pole?'
2nd: 'Yes.'
1st: 'Does the ice freeze your feet?'
2nd: 'Yes' (makes a shape).
1st: 'So you dance to keep warm?'
2nd: 'Yes' (does so).

Now change roles. It is not as daft as it sounds. Actor 1 makes suggestions; actor 2 does something physical with the suggestions. It is a basic co-operative impro: one partner pushes the action along and the other joins in. The second actor can't object to or resist any suggestion, but the suggestions aren't the second actor's responsibility, which gives a freedom to play and invent.

Exercise 2 – Yes and ...
This is the same as the last exercise except that the second actor adds a bit on, thus:

1st actor: 'Are you cold?'
2nd actor: 'Yes, and I'm going to light a fire.'
1st : 'And is it dark?'
2nd: 'Yes, and I'm able to see by the light of the flames.'
1st: 'Is something watching you?'
2nd: 'Yes, and I can see its eyes gleaming in the dark.'
1st: 'Are you frightened?'
2nd: 'Yes, and I'm digging myself into the snow.'

By adding the rule 'the second actor adds a bit' the game is given greater choices and therefore greater creative possibilities; *see* Chapter 6 to see how to develop the framework of an exercise to create many versions of a single exercise. In order to keep the game an actor's game rather than a writer's game, observe the following rules:

- Keep the game in the present tense: not 'I am going to dig a hole' but 'I am digging a hole', and act it out while you speak. Words and gestures help each other. It easier to find spontaneous words if your body is moving.
- Don't try too hard or you'll get tense and blocked. Play the game badly and often while you get used to it.
- Make sure you say 'Yes and' rather than 'Yes but'. The 'and' helps you to completely accept your partner's suggestions.

Exercise 3 – I'm lying
1st actor: (Makes an action, e.g. brushing teeth.)
2nd actor: 'What are you doing?'
1st: (Lies) 'I'm swimming.'
2nd: (Mimes the action of swimming.)
1st: 'What are you doing?'
2nd: (Lies) 'I'm fishing.'
1st: (Mimes the action of fishing.)
And so on.

The exercise creates a simple partnership where one partner instigates the action with words and the other joins in. Here the roles continually switch.

Using the 'Games' method outlined in Chapter 6, the possibilities are endless. For example:

1st actor: (Makes an action, e.g. brushing teeth.)
2nd actor: 'What are you doing?'
1st: (Lies) 'I'm swimming.'

The second actor now mimes the action of swimming. The first actor joins in. They create a 'swimming' impro, first without words, then using simple dialogue. When the impro has run its course, or run out, or the 1st actor has had enough:

1st actor: 'What are you doing?'
2nd actor: 'I'm fishing.'

They now improvise a fishing scene, and so on.

Here, the actors are using the exercise to cue a succession of simple impros. While you can make material from these exercises, their point here is to prepare you for an improvising workshop.

Body First, Words Follow
Unprepared verbal impros are always easier if the body is moving. The body is always speaking more powerfully than any words you can invent. Observe the rule that you only use words if they are strictly necessary.

Create a shape with your partner: a tableau that implies a relationship between you. Start to improvise with or without words. When you are both clear about the specific circumstances (neither of you may speak about the relationship – just play the scene) make another shape, do another impro, and so on. No impro should last more than half a minute. See how quickly you can set up circumstances and how many you can make without tensing up or rushing the scene.

Four Tips about Spontaneous Play
Not Trying to be Clever or Funny
Impro shows on television that edit out the failures and boring bits to imply that the improvisers are 100 per cent wildly funny suggest that improvisation must be funny to be worthwhile. This puts impossible pressure on beginners, and on the rehearsal space. In fact this sort of cleverness, creating finished theatrical moments at every turn, is good for instant performance but useless to the rehearsal process. By generating competitiveness between the actors, it destroys the creative space in which unexpected ideas can arise. You have to give up having to be funny. If something clever or funny drops out of air, well and good, but your job is to work attentively with your partner.

Two Improvisers and the 'Third Thing'
As you begin to improvise, if you are listening and responding to your partner rather than planning what you are going to say next, neither of you will be in total control of the material. Not being in total control is the essence of improvisation and depends on you being prepared to follow the material as it arises between you, rather than trying to control or 'write' it on your feet. Thus

OPPOSITE PAGE
Using physical relationship to trigger impro.

the 'third thing': the circumstances and characters arise through play, not through planning.

Improvisation Is Co-operative
Wherever the material takes you, whether into confrontation, rows, or scenes of hatred or abuse, you are always co-operating with your partner and they with you. Improvisation is always more akin to a dance than a fight. Remember also that the rehearsal space is safe. So long as you don't physically assault your partner you can say and do what you like to each other without having to suffer the consequences, as you would if you did these things in real life. Many of us like this aspect of theatre!

Breaking the Boredom Barrier
Games are usually played for pleasure and excitement, but to get the best out of games and exercises in terms of theatre, they need to be practised like musical scales. Even exercises as simple as those described above improve immensely with practice, so play them often until boredom sets in. Boredom is an important feature of creative impro, because once you know the game inside out, you can start to test it and manipulate it. Boredom is useful because it immediately generates curiosity – a true creative impulse.

Two Warm-Up Impros to Prepare for a Text Rehearsal
Repeat the Last Line – Listening and Responding
Learn to listen to your partner while improvising. It is easy to be too busy trying to think of clever or important things to say to listen to your partner. In fact, any conversation is a verbal improvisation, the difference being that conversations are not performances and are therefore less self-conscious.

Run an impro scene from a play in which you repeat your partner's last line before speaking your own. Integrate this so that the repetition does not sound out of place, but sounds natural.

Contact Impros
This exercise can be used for either spontaneous impro, scenarios or texts. You make a rule that you may not speak unless you touch. This takes practice, because the touching must look absolutely natural and must change with each new thought. For example:

1st actor: (While shaking 2's hand.) 'Good morning!'
2nd: (Puts arm round 1's shoulder) 'Do come in and sit down.'
1st: (Touching 2's hand) 'You have some news?'
2nd: (Putting hands on 1's shoulder) 'It's bad I'm afraid.'

The first actor has to make physical contact with the second in order to speak. However, speech is not necessary to continue the scene and both actors may choose to develop the scene silently. This exercise is very good for breaking up creaky old blocking or reviving over-rehearsed text scenes, but contact between the players is its most useful quality.

11 THE DEVISING ACTOR: SMALL GROUP WORK

THE JOY OF DEVISING

Most actors are cast in a very narrow range, so if your photograph says 'garage mechanic', 'comic mother-in-law' or 'nut boy', you may find that devising offers you an oasis of creative possibility in a desert of predictable bit-parts. Actors are not usually cast according to type for a devised show because the director doesn't know at audition precisely what characters will appear in the play. Good devising actors take the opportunity to make effective roles that show off their skills and strengths. Devising invariably gives you the chance to test and extend your range: you will use yourself more completely. Your relationship with other professionals and your role as an actor is likely to be less formal than in conventional situations. Above all, your personal experience, taste and professional judgements will actually be seen in the theatre piece that you are making.

THE ACTOR'S ROLE

Theatre is a co-operative art, but it does not follow that actors are naturally communal. A successful actor has to be able to socialize, but rehearsal for some is a private matter, and showing work in progress requires sensitivity and proper timing. Actors can be more vulnerable when they start rehearsal without a text. It follows that anyone casting a devising company needs to take the personal demeanour and preferred rehearsal style of individual actors into account.

Devising actors must be able to function well at a number of levels. Actors who are flexible in their working methods, have a liking for direct contact with the audience and have a fairly extrovert approach to rehearsal are likely to

---

The Devising Actor

- Enjoys collaboration and group work.
- Shows a natural professional optimism.
- Often has a range of performing skills, which may include music, dance, mime, clown, puppetry, internet scripting or storytelling.
- Has a constructively critical attitude to the rehearsal process.
- Uses criticism as a tool, using it to find the next step in the devising process.
- Has a strong interest in the physical languages of theatre, as well as text.
- Has a broad 'theatre-making' idea of the actor's role.
- Can cope with his or her role in the show remaining undefined until very late in the rehearsal process.
- Enjoys taking on a variety of acting and non-acting tasks in a production.

enjoy the devising process. Useful actors have a range of performing skills: music, singing and dancing are useful. Directors will also cast actors who, in addition to their acting skill, are effective team members and group-workers. A single company member who is destructively insecure can destroy a project.

THE ACTOR AND GROUP WORK

Group work is an important skill and can be learned. A number of early rehearsals will involve the actors working without the director in sub-groups, so the actor's skill is required to keep the process moving forward, to include everyone in the journey, and to take professional responsibility for the quality of the work produced by the group.

It is of course important to 'get on' with people, but the point is not to be nice, or have everyone like you, but to maintain a constructive, professional attitude that is generous and comprehensible to others. Much emotional energy is spent on group dynamics, often more than is given to the devising task. Difficulties and misunderstandings can set up additional rehearsal obstacles that damage the creative process and may destroy the show. The following tips might help you through the group work.

First Impressions
Try not to act on first impressions. Base your attitude on your experience of others rather than your expectation of what others will do. Work to create a positive impression of yourself in others as an open, cheerful, hopeful and demanding team member.

Giving to the Process
Everything starts with the actor. The best devising actors are those who 'have a go'. If you respond quickly and positively to a request to start an improvisation – even when the task is not clearly defined – you will always make a pos-

itive contribution to the devising process. This is true even if your attempt fails dismally, because by having a go you give others, including the director, permission to do the same. A 'dive in and see what happens' culture is very healthy, especially at the beginning of the process.

It Doesn't Have to be Perfect
A measure of devising actors is their capacity to tolerate mess. You cannot afford to wait until your work is good enough before showing it to others in the group. You have to let others see it 'warts and all'. At the start of the process everything is useful. All material creates comment and debate, exposes opinion and moves the process forward in very specific ways. In a devising rehearsal, there is almost certain to be a point where it seems impossible that a show will emerge from the plethora of ideas. Only experience can tell you that this is a normal part of the process.

Constructive Criticism
It is your job to offer constructive criticism when invited to comment on the work of others. Constructive criticism means that by clearly communicating your response to what you have seen, you suggest the way forward or the next step in the process. With practice, you will learn to say everything you feel about a fellow actor's work without them feeling attacked. You do this by learning to feed back in a positive, upbeat and rational way. If you cloud what you say with negative emotion – you sound angry, contemptuous or dismissive – your words simply won't be heard above your attitude.

Non-Collusion
Collusion happens when the comfort of the group becomes more important than achieving your work objectives. The unspoken agreement says 'I won't criticize/make demands on you if you don't criticize/make demands on me'. Collusion is the great potential pitfall of all creative

group processes. Actors are more vulnerable to it than most, because our need for love is so obvious. The temptation is to keep the group comfortable, rather than do the work. If your view of the group work is not that of your colleagues, it is important to be able to say it clearly. This may make you feel very lonely. The best way through is laughter: make your contributions very light, smile a lot, laugh, but stick to your guns!

Group Etiquette
- Turn up on time.
- It is your professional responsibility to be able to say 'no' as well as 'yes' when you are asked to take on work.
- If you agree to do something, do it, and do it on time.

LEFT: *Setting up the session.*
BELOW: *Early stage showing of work.*

Stages in the Devising Process and Your Role

Rehearsal	State of the Group/Production	Role of the Actor
First rehearsal	**Energy:** This is usually the time for the big picture, the moment when the director sets out a vision for the production Everything and everybody is new and exciting: the hard work hasn't yet started! Expectation is very high **Obstacles to work:** This is the first step into the unknown Sometimes actors are distracted by the need to impress each other or the director, and forget to listen to and note this seminal and important meeting	To put aside all preconceptions To be curious, open-minded and enthusiastic To contribute as required, being sensitive to the fragile nature of the group
First improvisations	**Energy:** This is the first opportunity for actors to show what they can do Professional relationships are new, challenging and vibrant **Obstacles to work:** *See* above Because relationships within the group have not yet consolidated, fear of failure or humiliation may mean that actors 'play safe' instead of genuinely exploring the task	To be able to respond to any request from the director To 'have a go', and fail with a good heart! To know your skills and strengths, to make them available when appropriate To work imaginatively, to take nothing for granted By working in an adventurous way you give others permission to do the same (sometimes including the director!)
Early work in small groups	**Energy:** Depends entirely on the small group dynamic There is a positive desire to get started **Obstacles to work:** Fear of failure and competition between members can block the work	To define and take on a role in the group that will make it effective; this could mean leading the group or waiting patiently for your turn
Sub-groups show each other work in progress	**Energy:** The first physical sense of the show Matters become more real to the whole group, which begins to feel like a company Actors watch each other at work, and aim to show themselves at their best **Obstacles to work:** It's possible to get bogged down in problems at this stage	To give complete focus of attention to the work of others To respond positively and generously to the work To praise all effort and achievement, to be clear and constructive in your criticism To respect the work of others and to expect the same in return

Rehearsal	State of the Group/Production	Role of the Actor
	This is where the company has to tolerate mess and have faith that consistent collective effort will produce a result	
Developing the work	**Energy:** At this stage creative energy feels very focused and specific Sub-groups may refine their work or everyone might develop one group's scenario The skills of individuals may be brought to bear on devising problems **Obstacles to work:** Technical issues and writing problems may stifle creative energy The company should revisit the original vision	To have ideas both for the show and for your own role To rehearse and develop those skills that the emerging show will demand
Framing the show	**Energy:** The director/actor relationship often becomes more conventional as the director moves into role, establishing distance and objectivity towards the emerging show Actors' energy becomes freed from the task of creating material and able to focus wholly on acting **Obstacles to work:** The relationships are starting to change The director's eye is clearly the final measure of choice	To work for the show rather than your part in it: the better the show the better you will look To create characters, relationships and transformations quickly and to order To place your bold choices before the director If necessary, to cheerfully discard work and try again
Conventional rehearsal	**Energy:** If the process gets this far you will have the luxury of focusing entirely upon your acting role You can begin to work in detail on characterization, text, narrative and any skills which your role requires **Obstacles to work:** Changing roles takes skill: you have to do it by agreement and know where the job stops If you cannot do this you will not be able to focus your role and give a strong focus to your performance	To bring your character to life as thoroughly as you can To give yourself completely to the play

- Every time you make a judgement on someone behind their back – negative or positive – you start to split the group. Avoid it.
- Acknowledge the contribution of others; celebrate and enjoy the achievements of others. Expect to receive the same for yourself from each member of the group.
- Assume others will always give the best they can. Expect that others will expect the best from you.

CREATIVITY WHEN REHEARSING IN SUB-GROUPS

The pressure is often considerably higher at every level if you have to create material in a small group or with a partner. What happens if you make nothing? Suppose your group's work is substandard? Suppose yours is the worst group? It is very unlikely that these will be issues unless your worry turns them into self-fulfilling prophecies. Groups may avoid committing themselves to a course of action and talk out their time, until they have to cobble something together at the last minute in order to show their work. Given the time pressure on most devising processes, the problem for the actor in a small group is to maintain the creative frame of mind under pressure to produce work within a tight timescale.

Freedom within a Framework

When you begin to work in a small group you will have already taken on a job, usually to create a scene together. Try to avoid slipping straight into rambling discussion, or getting into a mindset where you are already behind before you start. Plan a framework for your work together. How long do you have? Ten minutes? An hour? A day? What can be achieved in that time? Create an achievable objective. Break it into tasks if it is appropriate to do so. Freedom within a framework means that by defining and articulating the 'givens' you create a well-defined series

of achievable objectives. You are then free to focus all your creativity onto these objectives.

Creating and Letting Go

When you have an idea, and especially when you have committed yourself to it and brought it to life, it begins to feel like a part of you. If it is criticized or rejected, you are rejected. Because the process of devising is about throwing away almost everything and keeping almost nothing (if you're not throwing things away something is wrong!), you are bound to encounter this. Many actors talk about 'the work' for this reason, to give what they have made an objective, detached character, which makes it less personal if they have to change it or throw it away. You have to be passionate about what you have created but, like a writer, be willing to discard it whatever its fine qualities. In fact all work contributes to the quality, texture and richness of the final piece, whether or not it is actually used.

Discussing, Doing and Reviewing

Take steps to make sure you don't get trapped in endless talk. When you have an idea, find a way to try it out immediately, practically: the issues and problems then become concrete. You can observe and review what you've done, rather than what you might do, which is much more complicated! However awful your first efforts, you will still be moving forward. Even rejecting practical work is a step forward. Endless, frustrating talk usually comes from the fear of starting. All artists have the great problem of how to take the first step. The first step is a great commitment and is a step into the dark. The only way forward is to do it!

DOING IT – A BASIC SMALL GROUP WARM-UP

You can't really devise on your own. If you are doing this you are probably a writer or a performance artist. Devising actors will usually be

Small groups devising through improvisation.

working in a small group, either one alone or as part of a larger company. If you are working in a small group without a director and starting is a problem, use tableaux, body pictures and shapes to start yourselves off. These are statues or pictures made by two, three or more people, used to create moments or moods in a scene or representing the whole piece. Tableaux are ways of setting up a scene as a picture, where different players represent characters in the scene. They allow you to work silently, using a language of images rather than verbalized concepts. These are regressive and childish, and therefore very good for establishing a light, imaginative atmosphere in which simple play can take the group in a number of creative directions.

You may have been given a task – some prose, or an event to turn into theatre. Or you may be working on a short story, a myth or a fairy tale either as a warm-up or a project. This is an example of how you might work:

1. Break up the source material into several bits. If it is a story, each bit could be a significant point in the narrative. If a newspaper article, each bit could be a different person's point of view.

2. If you have no source you could start with moods: joy, grief, anger or love; life stages: birth, adolescence, courtship, decrepitude and death; the deadly sins: jealousy, lust, greed, etc.; or the virtues: faith, hope and charity. All these are very mediaeval!

3. Give each bit a title.

4. One actor stays out of the group and observes while the others make a tableau out of each title.

5. Rules of play are important here. It is a good idea to have a 'no talking' rule. The group works silently. The observer's job is simply to make the picture clearer by making adjustments to the body pattern – not to give an opinion.

6. Repeat the tableau until it can easily and accurately be re-created by the group.

7. Sequence the tableaux. If you are dramatizing a narrative the order of the tableaux will be obvious, or you may want to invent a less

obvious order at this stage. It is vital not to get into a discussion: to do so will kill the energy. Let the observer sequence the tableaux or, if all else fails, try sequencing as a group without speaking.

8. The group makes the first tableau, then the second, third and so on. You can play with the timing, taking up to, for example, half a minute to evolve the first tableau into the second. This slow change will give you a number of transitional pictures, possibly revealing moods and relationships. If you video the piece, you can freeze-frame moments and then expand them into scenes with dialogue.

The possibilities for play are now endless. You can:

• Freeze the movement between (for example) the first and second tableaux to create more tableaux and make the sequence more specific.

• Devise some narrative 'snapshot' tableaux between the original to make the narrative more specific.

• Ask the observer to narrate the action between tableaux.

• If the observer has a sense of rhythm, let them count in waltz time, rap time or whatever. Explore the possibilities for dance.

And so on.

This sequence might take half an hour, but is a much more efficient use of your time than starting with a discussion. You can now discuss the work in concrete rather than theoretical terms, and you will have started with the language of the body, which is the true language of theatre.

12 WORKING ALONE ON CHARACTER

EXERCISES FOR WORKING ALONE ON CHARACTER

Characters and characterization are discussed endlessly in rehearsal and the director will already have made important decisions before the actors are even auditioned. Characterization is fundamental to the production concept, and the director is likely to have cast you because you have qualities that help this interpretation. Nevertheless, however dictatorial the director's work, character development is finally the actor's responsibility. Directors will often talk philosophically or psychologically about characters. This is intellectually stimulating, but of little direct use to an actor. Relating the character's experience to the actor's is helpful because it helps the actor to empathize with the character. Imagery is useful too, since it helps the actor to contact the character using the senses rather than the intellect. Unless the director has been an actor or has trained actors, he or she is unlikely to tell you how to go about making a character. Whatever you make is, in any case, unique. You must decide what is right for your character. You will have to translate the discussions and conceptual instructions into action, and find ways in which you can work alone in order to bring fresh material to the next rehearsal. This chapter is to help you do that.

CREATING CHARACTERS FROM TEXT

If you have a text, study it thoroughly before starting to develop the character. Study will reveal the degree of detail with which the writer has imagined your character. If you are devising a play, for the purposes of this chapter use the research material as though it was text.

Take a notebook and rule out a form on each page with four columns under the following headings:

- Everything my character says about him/herself
- Everything anyone else says about my character
- Facts
- Notes.

First Exercise

Go through the whole text, highlighting in fluorescent marker pen all of your character's lines, and all instructions, entrances and business relevant to your character. As you work, note in the first column of your notebook everything the character says about him or herself – simply quote in the column what they say. It is important throughout this exercise to suspend judgement. You may get an immediate impression of the character. They may talk endlessly and compulsively about themselves or be absolutely silent. If the column remains empty it doesn't matter. You have still discovered something about the style of the play and about your character.

Second Exercise

Re-read the entire play, paying attention to all references made to your character by other characters. Highlight these references in a different colour. Again make no judgement. The comments may be prejudiced, they may be downright lies and they probably say more about the character speaking than your character. Never mind – put it all down. Perhaps no one mentions your character: that is also significant.

Third Exercise

Make a list of all the facts relevant to your character. Make no judgement. For example, if we consider Irena from Checkov's *Three Sisters*, it would be a fact that she is a young woman, the youngest of three sisters, but not that she 'wants to go to Moscow' – she only says that. Try to stick to objective matters. Most relationship dynamics are subjective, so leave them out. Write down only what is irrefutably true.

These lists create a sort of 'grid reference' to character decisions. The decisions you are able to make about your character must take account of this basic reference. You will quickly discover how tightly the character is drawn, and how much leeway the author has left you to build a character through your own decisions. The data yields not only characteristics but also sometimes the rhythm of the character in the text.

The 'Notes' column is for your own reflection once you have completed the exercises. Again, don't make judgements. The best use of this column is to ask questions about what is unclear or needs exploration in rehearsal.

Checklist

Begin to visualize the character by thinking through the total possible range of characteristics. For example:

- Physical characteristics, including age, height, weight, hair and skin colour, posture, physical build and type, mannerisms, voice, speech and speech mannerisms, dress and appearance.
- Psychological characteristics, including attitude: introvert/extrovert; type: intellectual/emotional/practical/intuitive; relationships: family/friends/lovers/ professional; maladjustments: obsessions/ phobias/superstitions; denied characteristics; self value: high or low; a winner or a loser?
- Cultural characteristics, including: class, working day, nationality, religion, politics, ethnicity, values and education.

This checklist can be endlessly extended, but characteristics are only of interest insofar as they help you, the actor, to transform into the character.

Your checklist will quickly show you what leeway the writer has left you to create the character from your imagination.

CHARACTER QUALITIES

When you have read the play a few times and completed the research analysis, you are ready to explore the qualities of the character You cannot study character without reference to a model of the human being. The model of man in this exercise assumes that we have an inner persona (hidden) and an outer persona (shown to the world), and that sometimes these two personae are in conflict. The model is quite old-fashioned, reminiscent of Freud's model of the conscious/unconscious human, or Descartes' model of the human body/soul dichotomy. However, the inner/outer dynamic is of great use in the dramatic exploration of psychological states, as long as we don't elevate the 'inner' at the expense of the 'outer'. This model assumes that characters have outer and inner qualities, which may or may not be the same. A character's outer life may in some respects mask a different secret inner life, and this secret life may be forced to the surface under pressure of external circumstances. The use of 'inner and outer' qualities is particularly useful when you are working on character alone, because there is often a dynamic – even a dialogue – between these conflicting qualities. The model is also highly theatrical, since character development becomes the revelation of inner secrets.

Exercise

This exercise asks you to list the inner and outer qualities of your character, paying attention to text research. Below, for example, some inner and outer qualities are listed for Lopakhin, the peasant boy who becomes *nouveau riche* through

Inner and outer qualities: Jocasta listening to Oedipus.

Lopakhin's Inner Qualities	Lopakhin's Outer Qualities
Vulnerable	Aggressive
Sensitive	Emotional
Frugal	Mean
Direct	Direct
Insecure	Clumsy
Controlling	Practical
Passionate	Demonstrative
Sincere	Sincere
Shy	Garrulous
Idealistic	Ambitious
Depressive	Ebullient
Class-loyal	Serf-loyal
Conservative	Materialistic

business and eventually buys the cherry orchard in Checkhov's play *The Cherry Orchard*.

In Act I of the play, Lopakhin says of himself 'I've got a lot of money but anybody can see I'm just a peasant, anyone who bothers with me at all and looks under my skin ...'.

There are many qualities to any character, far too many for one person to play, so be selective and choose those that strike you and help you to transform. For example, I have chosen the inner/outer dynamic of shy/garrulous to see what happens when Lopakhin has to engage with someone but lacks the words. Other qualities are consistent with his outer and inner states, and run right through him. When doing these exercises choose characteristics that are playable. You're not supposed to be a psychoanalyst, and if you were, it wouldn't help!

EXERCISES USING INNER AND OUTER QUALITIES

These are impros that give you an encounter with the character.

When working alone and unobserved it's easy to lose concentration and get lost, so keep the impro very short – five minutes maximum until you have begun to master the technique. If you can find a kindred spirit in the cast, watch each other and give feedback.

When constructing the exercise relate it closely to relevant scenes in the play. Give yourself the clear and simple objective of enriching your understanding of specific moments in the play. For example, if I were playing Lopakhin, I might want to create exercises that help me to understand his behaviour:

- In the first scene, when the family return to the Cherry Orchard.
- In party scene when he returns drunk, having bought the Cherry Orchard.
- During his last parting with Varia.

Making the Scenario

Imagine a simple scene, very close to the plot of the play, in which your character is alone, but is able to play an action (*see* 'Text, Action and Activities', page 85). For Lopakhin I would imagine him preparing to meet Ranyevskaia, who doesn't turn up. His action is to confront her with her financial circumstances. Give the

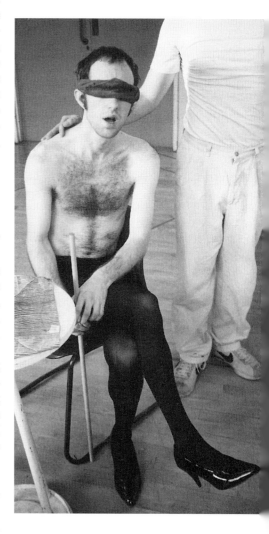

Tireisias rehearsing Oedipus Rex *in high heels and tights.*

character some activities (*see* page 88). Lopakhin might go over the figures, rehearse a speech or check his appearance.

Allow the character a single prop that encapsulates the character in the scene – I would give Lopakhin a heavy ledger. Give the character a single piece of costume that encapsulates the character in the play – I would give Lopakhin a stiff collar to fuss over.

Choose a piece of music that evokes the essence of the character. It is very important that this isn't 'mood music', which will distract you. For Lopakhin I would find the tune of a Russian peasant song, which I would learn.

Now play through the scene for a few minutes, using the activities to evolve the content. Don't play for too long. Stop and note anything significant that arises. Mark a beginning and an end moment for the scenario, and any useful moments in between. These might be realizations, mood shifts or impulses.

Replay a number of times, discarding 'padding' and irrelevance until you have an efficient series of activities making a scenario that would be an effective preparation for the role.

PHYSICAL TRANSFORMATION EXERCISES

Finding Images

Creating a character is not an intellectual exercise. While it starts with research and the collection of evidence, it is your intuition and imagination that will bring it alive.

Exercise: Imaging the Character

If my character were an animal, what animal would it be?

If my character were a colour, a precious stone, a fruit, a form of transport, an article of clothing, what would it be?

If my character were an hour of the day, a season of the year, a landscape, an element (earth, air, fire, water), what would it be?

Answer each question from the picture that arises in your mind, and not from a literal or logical answer. You are employing your imagination to find an image, which gives you a sense of the character. Again, you are looking for a 'hook' that excites or transforms you towards the character.

Animal Transformation

In this exercise you imagine an appropriate animal who shares essential qualities with your character. You observe that animal, either live, or on film or video. You transform physically into the animal.

Exercises in Animal Transformation

Choose a mammal, or at least an animal with roughly your number of arms and legs, and avoid pets. You want the animal in as natural a state as possible. Be specific about the character qualities you want to explore and try out some simple transformations before you make a choice. For an ebullient businessman you might choose a bear; a giraffe might give some of the qualities of a vicar; a doe for an innocent young girl; a camel for an old whore ... but these are cliché suggestions. The range of possibilities is huge, and the whole of a well-drawn, complex character cannot always be totally encapsulated by an animal exercise. However, you are looking for an imaginative 'hook' that you can repeat to find the sensation of the transformation.

Begin work on all fours so you get physically as far away as possible from yourself. Concentrate on inner and outer tempi: does your animal have a slow outer rhythm and a quick inner rhythm? Quick outer and slow inner rhythm? Or are the outer and inner rhythms the same, slow or quick? Watch the animal on video or at a zoo. Remember that caged animals experience conflicts irrelevant to their natures.

When you have established the animal transformation in terms of tempi, weight, their

THIS PAGE
TOP: *Animal transformation class, Catherine Clouzot at ArtsEd: how the room is prepared.*
ABOVE: *How the actors prepare.*

OPPOSITE PAGE
TOP: *Working alone in a common space.*
BOTTOM LEFT: *Shifting centre and weight.*
BOTTOM RIGHT: *Working with tempo.*

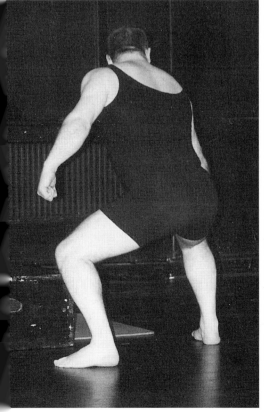

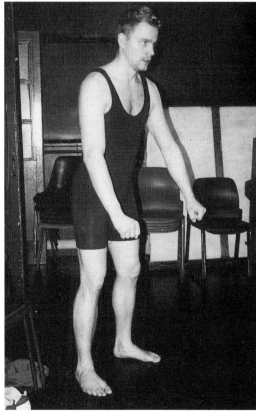

'centre' and some simple actions and responses, work with your animal in two contrasting moods, for example relaxed contrasted with fearful, or aggressive. Always work physically: try out a moment or a mood and make notes afterwards. The strength of this exercise is that it frees the body to work, so feel rather than think yourself through the sequence.

Isolate essences of your animal that apply to the character you are creating – a bear-like person, giraffe-like, swan-like. Work standing up. Use animal tempi, weight, centre of gravity, mannerisms and any other quality that 'hooks' you into character.

Levels of Acting in Animal Transformation
1. Explore transforming from yourself, into animal and into character. Don't immediately go all the way into character. Find some useful elements that please you.
2. Now create a series of simple activities – getting breakfast, running a bath, making tea and so on. Use your animal character elements and see how long you can sustain them.
3. Experiment with levels. If you play the animal qualities very strongly you will create a character that tends to the grotesque or the cartoon. A subtle use of the essences will give a more natural style. Which level you choose depends on the director's concept of the play.

Using Costume

Clothes change the way you feel, and alter the way you physically use yourself. Stanislavski famously described himself spontaneously transforming into Othello during an impassioned reading of the play, rehearsing alone in his room. He describes himself smearing his face, wrapping a bath towel round his head and striding round the room waving a loofah!

If you choose items of costume carefully, they can help you not only into the character but into the physical style of the period. For

example, a man rehearsing a restoration character might use a tight cummerbund and heeled shoes. A stiff collar encourages stillness in the head and adds to the authority of a character. Women often rehearse with a 'motley skirt'. This is a black cotton full wraparound skirt that falls from the waist to the ankles. Character shoes that are black, round-toed and have a low heel are also used.

WORKING ALONE ON CAMEO CHARACTERS

Making characters and transforming into other people is what actors do naturally. There is nothing to stop those who are between jobs from making and playing characters, which they could do without relying on writers, directors, agents or theatres.

Exercise in Costume Transformation

1. Find a piece of costume that makes you feel different and takes you towards your character. Collars, belts, wrist and headbands, skirts, cloaks, high heels, hats, spats can all be useful. Use two or three pieces at most.
2. Play a speech or a moment wearing the piece of costume, for example, a wing collar.
3. Now play the same moment without the collar, but maintaining the physicality.

The object is to internalize the physical sensation gained from this piece of costume.

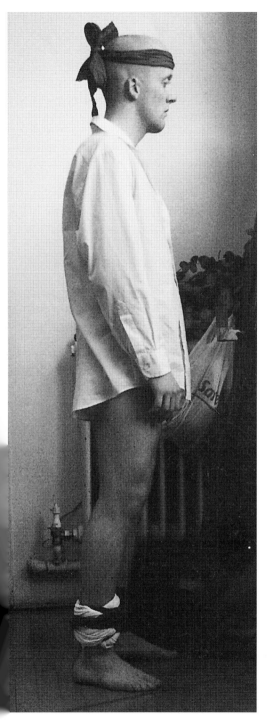

During the 1970s at Interaction Trust, we experimented with the idea of 'community cameos'. The idea was that an actor would revive a famous dead person, and have them walk the street, learning the ways of the twentieth century. Since then characters have sprung up in a range of settings from one-person shows to theme park performers to museum *animateurs*. The following notes may interest actors engaged in independent performance.

Making a Character from an Historical Figure

In 1976 I made a pilot community cameo project. The idea was to 'revive' a historical character who would live in Kentish Town and would learn about the twentieth century from local people. There would be a research and rehearsal period, followed by a 'performance' period during which the character would live in the community. The project would be entirely improvised – there would be no script of any kind. If performance arose, the character would improvise or prepare like any VIP at a public occasion. The character would literally learn how to survive in the modern world. Once the character had learned, for example, how to cross the road, they couldn't pretend not to know this in order to repeat a routine. I chose the nonsense poet Edward Lear (1812–88) who was also an illustrator, musician, traveller, diarist, teacher of Queen Victoria and friend of such eminents as Tennyson and Holman Hunt. Different historical periods yield different sorts of information. There is almost no information on Shakespeare for example – you would have to

*The author as Sir Neville Pratt (*Tales of Jungle and Farmyard, *1978).*

Edward Lear, 1976.

make him up by extrapolating from the lives of his contemporaries. Victorians like Lear, on the other hand, deluge the researcher with material because the leisured and semi-leisured classes of his period wrote copious letters and diaries. The project proceeded as follows.

First Stage: Research
Develop a daily routine that reflects the life of the subject: up at dawn, drawing on Hampstead Heath, copious diary writing, poetry, songs and music. Acquire small hand props such as quills and visit Lear's haunts, such as the parrot house at London Zoo – none of this in character.

Research: biographies, biographers, original material, paintings, letters and diaries, haunts, clothes. Also make detailed research of Victorian domestic life: lavatories, beds, heating, servants, eating and so on.

Second Stage: Rehearsal Routine
Begin transformation and storytelling rehearsals with the director, converting the research into conversation; we invent an account of (though not a rationale for) Lear's return.

Continue the daily routine out of character. All in-character rehearsals remain private. Begin to write letters as Lear to people still connected with him or his work (such as the curator of the Tate Gallery) and to friends who have agreed to participate. Relationships begin to develop through correspondence.

Streetwork.

Third Stage: Transformation and Emergence
The character is developed through conventional exercises. My rooms are converted gradually into facsimiles of Lear's rooms, with appropriate wallpaper, pictures and artefacts. The room, like the character, is an odd mixture of Victorian and modern features.

Friends and experts are invited briefly to tea in Lear's rooms, allowing conversational improvisation. These sessions are gradually extended. Entertainment during the sessions is as appropriate: drawing and singing.

Next the director takes 'Lear' into the world. We explore Chelsea – well known to Lear – at night and alone. Eventually some brief interactions take place, on the street, or in bars with members of the public.

Real costumes are now created, and real props and artefacts obtained. Everything must stand up to scrutiny!

Final Stage: Performance Routine
What would you do with a famous dead person who came back to life? We have engagements at events, educational conferences, art galleries, libraries and theatres. 'Lear' makes a daily routine walk, undertaken at the same time each day, passing by schools, shops, through a market, to the park to draw, and back home.

'Invitations to tea' provide another level of reality. Invitees, met on the street and in the market, turn up at Lear's rooms and find that there is actually tea, cucumber sandwiches and that 'we make our own entertainment'.

13 WORKING ON NARRATIVE AND RELATIONSHIPS

THE ACTOR GUIDES THE AUDIENCE

Theatre is a complex form of storytelling. This does not mean that all plays must tell stories; it means that the actor triggers a story in the imagination of the audience, and then does nothing inappropriate to disrupt the flow of that story in the minds of the audience. The great artist in the theatre is never the director or the actor, always the audience. The great actor subtly leads the audience into the narrative, sometimes nudging its collective imagination, sometimes letting it lead, never making one step inconsistent with the last, unless this is for deliberate effect. The actor leads the audience to the mountain top like a guide, and must therefore know where s/he is at all times, as well as the purpose of the journey.

ORIENTATION EXERCISE – EACH MOMENT HAS ITS STORY

This exercise demonstrates how any good actor reads a text: not as literature but as action. It helps you discover the story of your character at any moment in the play and it is easy to do alone. Use it to tell the whole story of your character's role in the play, or choose any of your character's moments in the play to play this exercise. Be specific when answering these questions, but don't intellectualize. Use your senses as the path to your imagination. Tell the story either for your role in the whole play, or for any scene or moment in it.

- **Where am I?** The environment, the setting of the play, or the setting in the moment. Experienced through the senses, for example a nineteenth-century middle-class drawing room: its gloom, the smell of polish, the crackle of the fire, the faint taint of smoke, the perfume of lavender, the dull gleam of a brass vase, the touch of satin, the nip of cold in the air ...

- **When is it?** Every sensual aspect of time: the season, e.g. the first day of spring, the depth of winter, blazing summer; and the hour, e.g. the witching hour, the darkest hour just before dawn, high noon, teatime. Consider also the immediately preceding moment and the moment that is to come.

- **What do I want?** This is your want or action: what you want from, or how you want to affect, another character in the scene you are playing. (This is discussed in more detail on page 88 under 'Working the Script'.) You might amend your action moment to moment, or it may stay the same depending on the circumstances and your fellow players. Make sure your choice is heightened and transitive, which means that it could be made physical – you could turn it into a gesture.

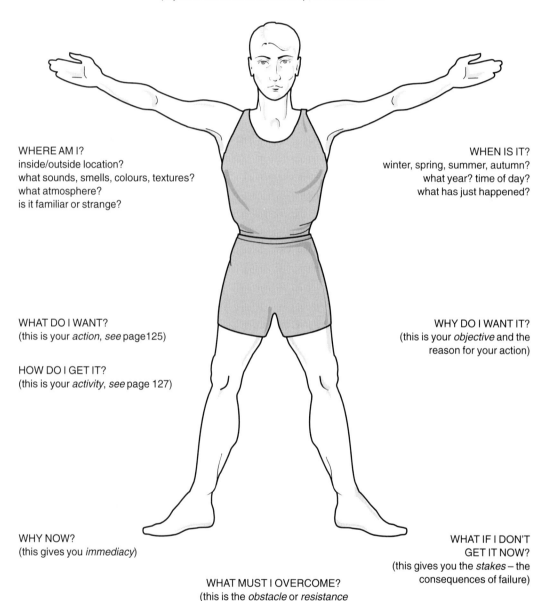

WHO AM I?
the character's background?
education? family? relationships?
social influences? taste, e.g. in clothes?
physical and emotional make-up, characteristics?

WHERE AM I?
inside/outside location?
what sounds, smells, colours, textures?
what atmosphere?
is it familiar or strange?

WHEN IS IT?
winter, spring, summer, autumn?
what year? time of day?
what has just happened?

WHAT DO I WANT?
(this is your *action*, *see* page125)

HOW DO I GET IT?
(this is your *activity*, *see* page 127)

WHY DO I WANT IT?
(this is your *objective* and the
reason for your action)

WHY NOW?
(this gives you *immediacy*)

WHAT IF I DON'T
GET IT NOW?
(this gives you the *stakes* – the
consequences of failure)

WHAT MUST I OVERCOME?
(this is the *obstacle* or *resistance*
and is your *problem* in the scene)

Psychological orientation.

126

- **Why do I want it?** This is the justification for your action. You don't have to make an intellectual argument for what your character does, but it does have to be consistent with the circumstances of the scene. When rehearsing a play, your job as an actor is to bend yourself to the text, not the other way round!
- **Why do I want it now?** The answer to this question ensures that your action is immediate, that it takes place now, onstage and not somewhere else.
- **What if I don't get it?** The answer to this question gives you the stakes. What is at stake in this moment? Your life? Your whole future? Your chance of happiness? Make the stakes high. The higher the stakes the greater the dramatic moment. Remember this is a play, not ordinary life.
- **How will I get what I want?** By doing what? These are your activities or tactics. Will you use charm, tears, brute force, emotional blackmail, plain speaking, cold politeness or some other social tactic to play your action?
- **What must I overcome?** The obstacle – what stands in the way of you achieving your action? It might be an inner obstacle – your conscience, for example. Or it might be an outer obstacle. The door is locked so you can't leave the room. Your outer obstacle might be another actor's action, which you have to overcome.
- **Who am I?** The answers to all of the previous questions give you the answer to that question 'in the immediate moment'.

REHEARSING ALONE USING NARRATIVE

The Script as Narrative – Breaking the Text into Units

Get to grips with the whole play (or the scenario, if you are devising) by dividing it into 'units of action'. A unit is a chunk of the play. In some plays it may conform to the 'beats' described in Chapter 9. Give each 'unit' a title. Sometimes the unit is tiny, sometimes it embraces several scenes. You might add a description of the unit including colour, tempo, weight, a sense of dark or lightness, or a scent – any sensual indication that evokes the atmosphere of the section for you.

There is no correct way to unit a play – no two people will do it in the same way, but as soon as you start to cut it up you will be struck by the individuality of the play's structure. A play like Genet's *Maids* is very easy to unit because it has a classical shape: a single plot in a single place, the action taking place more or less in real time. The same could be said of Sophocles' *Oedipus Rex*. Anything by Shakespeare, on the other hand is likely to be very difficult to unit, having plots and sub-plots, comic bits stuck in, scenes jumping from place to place, and so on. You may want to unit the plots and sub-plots in parallel in order to see how they weave together. Simple or complex, you will be immediately struck by the physical artistry of the piece. Your role is part of this structure, and you need understand it thoroughly so that you to take your place in the story.

Cartooning

If you are working with others, develop your uniting skills through simple cartooning. First create a group picture – a tableau that expresses the title of the scene. Be aware of your choices of style at this stage. You can work entirely on the events in the story – the material. However, the world of the play might lend itself to titles expressed as a series of political slogans, emotional outbursts, religious commandments or graffiti. The style you give to the titles reflects the style of the writing and the style of the group pictures you create.

Run through a succession of units, physicalizing each title, that is making a picture of each title using your bodies, until you get the sequence smooth and accurate. Either let one of the group watch you for accuracy or work in front of a mirror. The purpose of the exercise is for everyone to thoroughly understand the sequence of events and the tone of the play. Physicalizing the titles helps you to get this understanding beyond your brain and into your body.

How you develop the exercise depends on the play. If the structure of the play is simple (classical structure), you can unit all of it. You might unit plays with sub-plots (Shakespeare for instance) as a series of stories, disentangling them and narrating each from beginning to end. The company may wish to focus on a short but complex section of a play to make sure that everyone is clear about how each of them fits into each moment of the action.

Increase the detail and specificity of the exercise by creating subtitles between the titles, putting a title to each subtitle and physicalizing these. Now take any two unit titles and narrate the story of the play as it occurs between those titles. If you work alone, record yourself, replay and revise. Just do this for the parts of the play that are unclear to you.

If you are working with a small group of colleagues, tell the story to each other. For example, let one person start and the others fill in as though remembering the detail as the story unfolds. Play 'finish the sentence', that is, tell the story by one person starting a sentence and the next person finishing it. Then they start the next sentence and another completes it, and so on. This exercise emphasizes that the group is learning together, and creates a 'telepathic' atmosphere among the players.

When you have enough tableaux you can begin to cartoon sections of the narrative by moving smoothly from one picture to the next so the cartoon develops like an old fashioned 'flicker book' – movement being created from a sequence of stills. Keep the style of the play in mind as you start to cartoon.

This whole exercise works best if it is recorded and displayed, preferably on the rehearsal room wall, so that it helps to transform the rehearsal space to one focused entirely on the production. You can obviously display the titles; you might photograph each tableau and display it with the title.

Rehearsing through Stories

To storytell a moment, your scene or a whole play, is to explore a piece of theatre from the point of view of its events. It is easy to drown in your own emotional moment and forget that a play is a story communicated simultaneously on many levels. Storytelling is communal, and therefore a very good company-building technique for actors working without a director. You can storytell and act out; you can insert tableaux as 'still photographs'; you can storytell into a scene, then play out the scene and continue the story; or

Cartooning the relationship.

you can play a scene in which, the moment the scene goes 'off' or freezes up, you go back to telling the story.

Storytelling allows you to work with an overview of the whole play or scene, not just your own bit of it, so it places your individual work in context. Narrative also takes a more distant perspective on its material, and this perspective makes the material easier to control, which is very useful during early rehearsal.

Using Different Tenses in Getting to Grips with Narrative

Use different tenses when telling your character's story. The past tense reconstructs events, so you can tell as though remembering. The future tense plans what will happen. Both give you good control over the material, so they are very useful at the beginning of rehearsal when you are getting to grips with the text. While you are learning to create the narrative thread of the plot from your character's point of view, the past tense is useful. Later in the rehearsal process, the present tense is more useful because it is emotional, immediate and dramatic – you are in the swim of events. You don't know what will happen – you are part of the shape of what is happening, and not entirely in control.

The Story of the Relationship

The feeling that something is about to happen is what stops an audience from walking out of the theatre. Any point of change has dramatic potential, whether this is a twist in the plot or character development. The currency of narrative on stage is relationship development. It is invariably through this development that the story is told. The twists of the plot engage us, and we are riveted by those moments when external or internal factors conspire to reveal or uncover hidden character traits, or to shift the dynamic of a relationship.

Before you begin work on relationships, you must be thoroughly familiar with your

The storyteller as 'messenger', emotionally disturbed by the story.

129

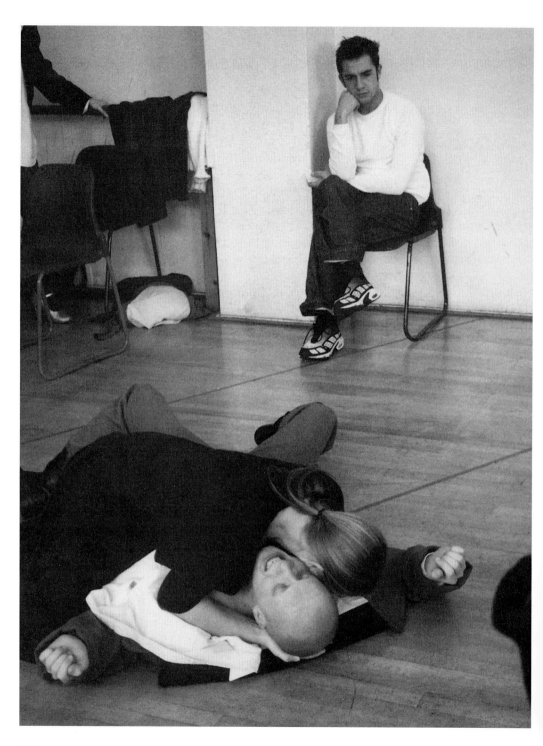

OPPOSITE PAGE & RIGHT
Telling the story using physical action.

character, and so have made and worked through your character decisions with the help of Chapter 12.

As you develop your character you will discover objects you associate with the character. These character objects – elements of costume, personal things in the form of practical props and intimate objects that trigger the characterization in the actor, such as a locket, photograph or ring – can be used in relationship exercises.

The Pitfalls of Working without the Director

If you are rehearsing a text make sure you stay within the frame of reference of the play. Above all, avoid introducing arbitrary material. Do not, for example, discover through improvisation that your character had traumatic experiences, or has developed eccentric foibles not referred to in the play, which totally govern his motivation. Instead of solving problems, you will have created new ones for yourself and everyone else.

Through improvisation you are creating a context for the scenes you are going to play. This context must in no way impair or limit the choices you can make when playing the scene.

How to Set Up an Exercise

As always, work to clear objectives and seek to solve clearly defined problems. You may wish to create the previous circumstance of a scene, or to explore aspects of your relationship with another character in order to make bolder and clearer choices in the play. This context is of no interest to the audience, so don't be tempted to display it. The actor has to know more than the audience does to be confident and clear, but this knowledge must never muddy the work of the writer whose skill lies precisely in knowing what to leave out.

Choose the exact moment you want to improvise, then answer all of the questions asked in the orientation exercise at the beginning of this chapter. This will give you a very specific framework for the exercise.

Work briefly – about five minutes – and adjust your answers to the orientation questions until you are satisfied that your answers are accurate, relevant, practical and dramatic.

Context Exercises

For this exercise you choose a moment of significance to the play that is referred to in the play but does not feature as a scene. You bring that moment to life with your partner. Remember that you are not trying to write another play, or trudge through every moment in your character's life. The object is to bring life to the scene and this often means bringing to the senses moments that are memorable and significant to your character, so that you can create a context, believable to you, for your character's action.

Realistic plays lend themselves strongly to this approach – the plays of Ibsen and of his modern exemplar, Arthur Miller, write about people whose lives are bound down by relationship incidents in their past. In Ibsen's *Little Eyolf* or Miller's *All my Sons*, both plays revolve entirely around a single incident not scripted, but entirely controlling the action. Some writing styles will give you nothing of the context, history or circumstances of a relationship, reducing the actor to intuitive guesswork when making decisions. Simple context impros can help the actor's decision-making process, by profiling questions that wouldn't otherwise arise. In this case choose simple incidents to improvise, but connect them to a phrase, expression or inference that actually occurs in the text. The idea is to add layers to your characterization and relationship. To do this, the text must trigger and recall the sensations generated by the impro.

Previous Circumstances

In this exercise you are exploring the moment that actually gets you onto the stage, the moment in the story just before the scene that you have to play. The exercise strongly connects the 'who, what, how, where', described on pages 125–6, to the text. The purpose of the exercise is to motivate or justify your action in the scene, and this must be strongly in your mind when you invent the impro. Remember that your aim is to strengthen the action of the scene, not to write another play.

Relationship Exercise

Combine the exercises suggested in this chapter to create relationship exercises:

1. Begin by researching the text – if there is one – for all references to the relationship by the characters or by others in the play.
2. Write down all relationship facts given in the script or scenario, for example parent/child, brother/sister, master/servant relationship.
3. Create some images for the relationship. For example is it:

   • Distant, close, intimate?
   • Hot, warm, tepid, cold?
   • Sweet, bland, spicy, sour?

And so on.

4. How does your character feel on meeting the other? For example is it

   • Like sinking into a warm bath?
   • Like having a flea dropped down your pants?
   • Like being fitted into a straightjacket?

And so on.

5. Devise a situation within the world of the play that will allow you to explore your relationship to your partner.
6. Answer all the orientation questions at the beginning of this chapter for the situation you have devised.
7. Play through the exercise with your partner, both in character.
8. Repeat, revising and developing your choices.
9. Devise a new situation that will allow your partner to explore their character's relationship with your character.

14 THE REHEARSAL OF EVERYDAY LIFE

Sustaining a career in the theatre depends to some extent on your ability to continue to function when there is no pressure to do so, in other words when you are out of work. Because rehearsal is such an intense experience, and the resulting run of a play is often not very long, you can sometimes feel dropped out of an emotional rollercoaster into a void of inactivity. Unless you keep active, you may not be physically and vocally fit to pick up the chance that suddenly and unexpectedly offers itself.

Out of work often also means on your own – at least on a professional level – unless you work with a workshop or have access to an actors' centre. Actor communities are characteristically unstable, and it is useful to develop an independent routine that you can easily pick up between jobs.

In one sense an actor's whole life is rehearsal, consisting of rehearsing shows and preparing for the next job. If you come out of work, get depressed and vegetate, then you are rehearsing going to pieces, becoming less alert, less skilled and less employable. The reverse is also possible. You can literally 'rest' actively by replenishing your resources and feeding yourself with whatever may come in useful in the future from books, galleries, concerts, personal projects, and so on.

The concept of 'lifelong learning' is not new to actors, who have always engaged in study and development spanning the whole of their life. An actor ingests material on an intellectual, emotional and physical level in rehearsal and in life. Furthermore, the rhythm of the life swings creatively between the 'action' of rehearsal and performance and the reflection of the resting period.

PATTERNS, BLOCKS AND RECOVERY – A PERSONAL AND PROFESSIONAL RECORD

Keep a diary. If nothing else, once you're famous it will help the autobiography! A professional diary is written regularly, irrespective of work pressure and to a format that exposes patterns of personal and professional behaviour. It is a sort of dialogue with yourself. The diary validates and witnesses your work. Acting is a totally ephemeral art: as soon as you do it no evidence remains – it has disappeared. It is very easy to get lost and to forget what makes your working life tick.

Take exactly the same attitude to each working day, whether you are in or out of work, on a West End stage, developing work on your own or working in a restaurant. Integrate your diary with the work. Commit yourself simply to writing something each day, if only a couple of sentences. The ritual is as important as the activity. Once the habit is established it becomes a small ritual in which you stop and reflect, however briefly, on what is happening to you.

133

The Professional Record

The professional record contains personal, professional and technical material, and it is important that this exercise doesn't degenerate into maudlin navel-gazing. The record must also be clear and easy to access, otherwise its value as a reference will be lost: an A4 hardcover lined book is very suitable. Make sure it is dated. The record is personal and confidential: if you write a record to be read to or to impress a third party, this will become a distraction to the record. For this reason, don't gossip about yourself by discussing the log unless you have a specific professional reason for doing so.

One way of arranging the material is to score across two pages under the headings described below, with a row each for incidents, reflection, response and behaviour patterns. If you write a lot, one double page will serve for a day. If not, use a double page for a week.

Incident Log

Use this section to record simple observations of your own and others' behaviour. Observing and recording is fundamental to the actor's craft, just as sketching is fundamental to the visual artist: something happens and you file it for future use. Finding your own way of doing this takes practice, and the two common mistakes are essay-writing and missing the point. You end up writing reams of boring drivel and you've given up after a week.

Practise finding the essence of an incident and recording it in just enough words so that it triggers your ability to recall it.

For example:

- An incident on a crowded tube train was recorded – three people manoeuvring for a single seat without talking to each other or making eye contact.
- One diarist collected a glossary of idioms used by friends and colleagues.

- A diarist noted every day a single moment when ordinary life came nearest to theatre.
- A diarist regularly visited a criminal court, the casualty ward of a hospital or a police station, noting incidents as theatre under the headings costume, character, ritual and plot.

Reflective Log

The incident section is a jumble of events, personal and professional, concerning you and others. In the reflective section you select a moment that gives you pause for thought. It might be a personal or professional insight, or a connection may have come to light. You record that you have become conscious of something.

Artist's Response

This is a blank space in which you respond to an incident. You have to use words because there's no room for anything else (but *see* 'The Scrapbook' below); here you express the moment in a way that is neither an argument nor an essay. It might be an image or a snatch of poetry, your own or someone else's, even a memo or a slogan written to yourself.

Professional Patterns

In this section you begin to discover your professional habits that seem to recur in rehearsal. Observing your own patterns sharpens your ability to observe others, and this is a fundamental actor's skill: it also helps you to become conscious of behaviour that gets in the way of your work, and gives you a chance to become aware of and control the outcome of the pattern. For example:

- A diarist discovered that she became physically tense when her work was criticized, and she could remember the comments afterwards. She trained herself to become aware of and to release the tension as it occurred. This improved her listening powers.

- A diarist became aware that his interest in his work depended on his relationship with the director. He would engage when he felt liked and withdraw when he felt ignored of unloved. He learned to recognize this pattern and laugh at himself.
- A diarist could never quite finish his work. Everything remained a 'rough' or a 'draft'. He found it emotionally difficult to present finished work for fear of a critical judgement on it.
- A diarist recorded a pattern of emotional blocks in rehearsal, occurring when the feeling was tender or vulnerable.
- A diarist noted her habit of 'holding on' to her mistakes, adopting a destructively self-critical attitude towards her work.

THE SCRAPBOOK: A RECORD USING IMAGERY

Yourself as a Character

The scrapbook complements the diary as a personal record. The technique is the opposite of the diary. In the diary you observe yourself as though you were a character and you create a record of yourself exactly as though you were developing a character. Look at some of the exercises in Chapter 12 and apply them to yourself as though you were a character. You will have to work on detachment. Although you have more information on yourself, and more evidence than on anyone else, it is very difficult to see yourself clearly without finding a psychological observation point, and that takes practice. The pay-off for the actor is that by using a creative technique you can look at yourself professionally without descending into psychobabble or intellectual analysis, neither of which are helpful.

The Scrapbook

The technique is to create a scrapbook. Buy or make a proper scrapbook that has big sheets of different-coloured sugar paper. Pages should be big – A3 at least. You use a single or double page for a project, and each project is a collage of materials: some photographs, a poem on a scrap of paper, cuttings from papers or magazines, two-dimensional objects of all kinds, all of which have emotional resonance for you. While the professional log is organized, sequential and analytical, the scrapbook exercises the emotions and the intuition, and therefore has a feeling of randomness. Basic equipment for keeping a scrap box includes:

- scrapbook
- adhesive
- paintbox and brushes
- coloured pens and pencils
- scissors
- craft knife.

The Language of Imagery

The scrapbook allows you to create a language through objects, images, colour, texture, spatial relationships, words, letters, line, numbers and so on. Choose a personal theme and create a collage of these and other appropriate objects on the page. This is child's play and hopefully will help you recover the childlike sensations so vital to creative work. The habit of regular recourse to imagery will help you build a path into the imagination other than the physical and verbal paths so far described. The scrapbook is an effective warm-up into an imaginative, creative or devising exercise. The language of imagery is less specific and less technical than that of words, communicating on a number of levels that are emotional rather than logical. The decision-making process, including when and how often you do it, is very much to do with what feels right.

Each double page of the scrapbook looks like a collage, and may include poetry, documents, cuttings, tickets, and letters – anything not too thick that you can stick to paper. Popular scrapbook themes include identity, childhood, favourites and birthday.

AFTERWORD: THE SOUND OF A PENNY DROPPING

This book is full of suggestions of things to do. The plans, exercises, workshops, and schedules that fill it are vital to rehearsal because they provide the framework for creative interaction, out of which moments of understanding arise. However, it is these moments and not the framework that are the real stepping stones of rehearsal.

In the rehearsal room I discover the beauty and precision of a playwright's language and the clumsy inadequacy of my own. It isn't that I can't make myself understood; finding words isn't the issue, but how to convey a simple idea so that it can be completely heard. In the theatre understanding must go right inside the actor, because it is the actor's whole being that finally speaks to the audience. A moment of understanding happens to a performer, a director or into a whole company of actors when they suddenly know something that they previously understood only intellectually in the head. Actors know that they have to 'hook' into the character and fear that they might not be able to do so. This is one of the actor's recurring nightmares. This 'hook' is often caricatured or derided. The 'actress must find her shoes!' is simultaneously an indulgence and the truth. Actors really do have to find the prop, the garment, the smell, the hint, the illuminating instant, the philosopher's stone, the moment of satori – whatever it takes, after which they can sit comfortably inside the being of another person. These moments are not logical, do not respond to concentration, application, hard work or diligent practice, and cannot be hunted down by means of progressive acting exercises. They are moments of grace, and all that the rehearsal space can do is to maximize the chance that they will happen.

These creative moments, the moment when the penny drops, are simultaneously unforgettable and impossible to record. No one says anything. We are simply aware that something may have happened. The moment is usually very small. Directors and especially acting teachers are in the habit of claiming rehearsal 'breakthroughs': this is an attempt to dramatize the moment and claim a bit of it for themselves, but these apparently dramatic steps forward are usually followed by equally dramatic steps backward. Real progress is invariably tiny, subtle and all-pervasive.

The creative moment is a living thing and, as with other living things, the way to develop it is to 'use it or lose it'. You have to know that something has happened, acknowledge it, and constantly refer to it in order fully to establish it in the imaginative world of the play. This is difficult to do because subtle relationships are involved. First, the actor must have a healthy relationship with his or her own growth and development. Behaviour, insight and actions that are 'out of character', and that are the stuff of personal progress in rehearsal, must be completely accepted by the actor to have lasting effect. Second, a

Pennies dropping.

creative relationship between the actor and the director is needed that allows the director a 'mid-wifing' role in the birth of a creative incident. The director must be intuitive and sensitive enough to know when the actor is on the brink of such a moment, and avoid getting in the way.

From the director's point of view, creative progress begins life as a creative problem. A moment in the play is not working properly, or is unfulfilled or incomprehensible. There is a temptation to hammer at the problem, trying to force it to come right. This is invariably a mistake because the problem is rarely where you think it is. Often the presenting difficulty is only a symptom of a mistake that has happened elsewhere, or is endemic to the production. The director must feel a way into the problem, either from elsewhere in the play or off the text altogether. The problem is experienced as a 'block', meaning a block to the energy of the play. Once the block is solved, energy can flow again.

These are elements of the life of the play. The play is literally created in rehearsal: a living thing, because without the spark of life no text or production, however technically brilliant, means anything at all.

BIBLIOGRAPHY

REHEARSAL THEORY IN HISTORY AND NOW

Konijn, Elly A., *Acting Emotions* (Amsterdam University Press, 1997)

Mamet, *True or False* (Faber, 1998)

Mostyn (intro), *Shakespeare's First Folio (introduction)* (Applause, 1995)

Rudlin and Paul (ed. and trans.), *COPEAU texts on theatre* (Routledge, 1990)

Stanislavski, C., *Building a Character* (Methuen, 1950)

Styan, *Restoration Comedy in Performance* (Cambridge University Press, 1986)

Taylor, George, *Players and Performances in the Victorian Theatre* (Manchester University Press, 1989)

Wiles, *Greek Theatre* (Cambridge University Press, 2000)

PSYCHOLOGY OF PLAY

Bettleheim, Bruno, *The Uses of Enchantment* (Penguin, 1987)

Opie, Iona and Peter, *The Lore and Language of Schoolchildren* (Paladin, 1982)

Winnicott, D. W., *Playing and Reality* (Routledge, 1982)

GAMES IN PRACTICE

Barker, Clive, *Theatre Games* (Methuen, 1977)

Boal, Augusto, *Games for Actors and Non-actors* (Routledge, 1995)

Johnstone, Chris, *House of Games* (Nick Hern, 1998)

IMPROVISATION

Checkov, Michael, *On the Technique of Acting* (Harper Collins, 1991)

Coveney, Michael, *The World According to Mike Leigh* (HarperCollins, 1997)

Johnstone, Keith, *Impro – Improvisation and the Theatre* (Methuen, 1979)

Spolin, Viola, *Improvisation for the Theatre* (NW University Press, 1984)

ACTORS IN REHEARSAL

Berkoff, *Graft: Tales of an Actor* (Oberon, 1999)

Cole & Chinoy, *Actors on Acting (Personal Accounts through History)* (Crown Publications, 1976)

Gordon, Mel, *The Stanislavsky Technique Russia (A Workbook for Actors)* (Applause, 1987)

Huston, *The Actor's Instrument* (Michigan University Press, 1992)

Lecoq, Jacques, *The Moving Body* (Methuen, 1997)

Oida, Yoshi, *The Invisible Actor* (Methuen, 1997)

Rudkin, John, *Commedia dell'Arte (An Actor's Handbook)* (Routledge, 1994)

Suzuki, Tadashi, *The Theatre Writings of ...* (TCG, 1985)

Young, Jordan R., *Acting Solo* (Apollo Press, 1989)

DIRECTORS IN REHEARSAL

Appia, *Actor, Space, Light* (Calder, 1982)

Braun, Edward, *The Director and the Stage* (Methuen, 1982)

Brook, Peter, *There are no Secrets* (Methuen, 1993)

Leiter, Sam, *The Great Stage Directors* (Facts on File, 1994)

Leonard, Charles, *Michael Checkov's 'To the Director and the Playwrite'* (Limelight, 1984)

Spolin, Viola, *Theatre Games for Rehearsal (A directors Handbook)* (Northwestern University Press, 1985)

Wagner, Betty Jane, *Dorothy Heathcote Drama as a learning medium* (Hutchinson, 1979)

THEATRE MAKERS

Coult and Kershaw, *Engineers of the Imagination* (Methuen, 1990)

Mason, Bim, *Street Theatre and other Outdoor Performances* (Routledge, 1994)

Watson, Ian, *Towards a Third Theatre Eugenio Barba and the Odin Teatret* (Routledge, 1993)

THEATRE PRACTICE

Barker, H., *Arguments for a Theatre* (Manchester University, 1993)

Bennett, S., *Theatre Audiences* (Routledge, 1990)

Berkoff, S., *Graft: Tales of an Actor* (Oberon, 1999)

Blau, H., *The Audience* (John Hopkins, 1990)

Fenner, Jill, *The Actor's Handbook* (Bloomsbury, 1998)

Hanna, J.L., *Performer–Audience* (University of Texas Press, 1983)

Hayman, R., *How to Read a Play* (Oberon, 1999)

Schumacher, C., *Artaud on Theatre* (Methuen, 1989)

Stafford-Clark, M., *Letters to George* (Hern, 1989)

INDEX